Dear Josh

A.K.A

aka,

101 MANTRAS
FOR LIFE

Ben Wardle x

BEN WARDLE

"The most attractive thing you can ever wear is authenticity" – Ben Wardle

Also by Ben Wardle

Live Your Best Life – 50 essays on authenticity, confidence and resilience.

Road to Recovery – Surviving anorexia, embracing my sexuality, and transforming my life.

For signed copies of all Ben Wardle's book titles: www.benwardle.org/shop

THE 101 MANTRAS

INTRODUCTION

Dear reader,

A very warm welcome to my first collection of '101 mantras for life'! I hope that you might find the mantras, ideas and reflections that follow to be a source of inspiration and empowerment as you go about your daily life!

The word 'mantra', which originates from the Hindu and Buddhist schools of thought, is literally translated as 'instrument of thought'. Thus, the 101 mantras that follow are best understood as a collection of thoughts and ideas for how to live your best life. They are statements and slogans that can be returned to and repeated frequently, offering you a sustained source of inspiration and insight as you journey through this world.

You might find that some of these mantras don't speak to you – you may even find that there are a couple you don't personally agree with! And that's okay! Each of us is on our own unique journey through life, with our own unique set of core values and moral principles. And so, whilst I hope that a couple of these mantras might speak to you and inspire you, my greatest hope is that this collection of ideas will encourage you to think more deeply about what brings you happiness, meaning and fulfilment in your life as an individual.

Every single one of us is the master of our own destiny. We alone are in charge of what we do, believe and stand for as human beings. And so, we must dare to take responsibility for our own lives and we must dare to live each day as our most fearlessly authentic selves. I sincerely hope that the mantras in this collection will give you a little bit of inspiration and motivation to do just that.

I hope that you enjoy reading and reflecting on the mantras in this collection. I hope that you might find a couple of 'pearls of wisdom' to inspire you whilst you go about your daily life as a human being! At all times, remember that life is about progress and not perfection. And at all times, remember to try to enjoy the journey! Whatever's going on in your life right now, I urge you to keep going and keep growing!

Thank you so much for your kindness and support. I genuinely could not appreciate it more. Please keep in touch and keep living your best life. You are amazing! With all my love, Ben

1 DO WHAT MAKES YOU HAPPY

'The purpose of our lives', says the Dalai Lama, 'is to be happy'. Every single human being wants one thing in life – to be happy. And every single human being – including you - deserves to experience and achieve this happiness! That's right; you deserve to be happy!

And here's the good news: the power to experience and achieve this happiness is completely within your own very hands! To quote the Dalai Lama again: "Happiness is not something readymade. It comes from your own actions". This is very good news indeed because it means you are more than capable of achieving deep, genuine and long-lasting happiness in this lifetime.

Let us turn once more to wise words from the Dalai Lama, who says this: "Happiness is a state of mind. With physical comforts, if your mind is still in a state of confusion and agitation, it is not happiness. Happiness means calmness of mind".

Happiness means following your heart and fulfilling your potential. It means living life on your own terms as an authentic, confident and resilient human being. Strive to be a person of courage, not conformity. Live your life with individuality, integrity, and with an aspiration to inspire others to do the same. This is your one and only lifetime, and so you deserve to live it to the full as the very best version of your most authentic self!

John Stuart Mill, a strong supporter of individual autonomy, argued that we ought to live our lives in accordance with the 'non-harm principle'. This is the idea that you are free to do whatever makes you genuinely happy and fulfilled in life, as long as you are not causing harm to other people.

Whilst other people are entitled to offer you advice or guidance, nobody has a right to prohibit your self-expression for any reason other than to prevent harm being caused to other people. In other words, as long as you are not causing anybody else any harm, you have the right to do absolutely whatever – and be absolutely whoever - makes you feel genuinely happy and fulfilled.

Jacob Nordby puts it like this: "You know how every once in a while you do something, and the little voice inside you says 'There. That's it. That's why you're here'…and you get a warm glow in your heart because you know it's true? DO MORE OF THAT!"

Let me say that once more: whatever it is that makes you feel 'that's why I'm here'…DO MORE OF THAT! Do more of what makes you genuinely happy! Happiness is available to you, right here and right now! As Abraham Lincoln famously said, 'most folks are as happy as they make up their minds to be'. By choosing to live an authentic and meaningful life filled with love, you can consciously choose to be happy!

So make it your mission to live every day with absolute authenticity! Know that you deserve a lifetime of happiness and fulfilment. Do more of the things that make you happy and live every single day as the unique individual that you were born to be! Live your life on your terms and make your happiness your absolute priority!

2 DO WHAT'S RIGHT FOR YOU

This is your life, and you deserve to live every single second of it on your own terms. Instead of spending your life people-pleasing and conforming, commit yourself to living a fearlessly authentic and genuinely fulfilling existence!

Of course, there are undoubtedly many situations when it may be necessary to make certain compromises or small sacrifices for a greater good. And I'm not suggesting you should do whatever you want at the expense of other people's health, happiness or wellbeing.

However, what I am saying is that you cannot live your life as a slave to other people's opinions, wishes, or expectations. You cannot afford to lose sight of your authentic identity for the sake of pleasing or impressing other people. And you cannot compromise on living your best life in order to conform to the opinions of utterly irrelevant outsiders!

Stop depending on external validation. Stop being so addicted to people-pleasing. Stop worrying about upsetting people or letting people down! Instead of living your life in accordance with what society, your parents or your peers want, live life on your own terms! Get fearless about doing what's right for you, without a single drop of guilt!

At the end of the day, this is your life. As long as you are not causing harm to anybody, then you have absolutely nothing to apologise for! You were not put on this planet to conform and people please! You were put on this planet to find happiness and thrive as an autonomous individual! And that means living life on your terms!

So stop worrying about other people's opinions or expectations! Instead, you need to focus on thinking about what you actually want out of life! Ask yourself this: What kind of life do you want to live? What kind of person do you want to be? What values and principles are most important to you as an individual? What hobbies, interests and career paths bring you the greatest amount of happiness?

Don't feel bad about doing what's right for you. Remember that you are the master of your own destiny! Live every second of your existence on your own terms as an autonomous individual, not a slave to society or a prisoner to other people's opinions!

You were not put on this planet to just conform or fulfil other people's expectations. Instead, you were put on this planet to shine and thrive as the very best version of yourself! Never feel bad about doing what's right for you—never apologise for making your mental health and personal wellbeing your priority.

At the end of the day, only you know what is best for you. And at the end of the day, the only person you need to answer to is yourself! And so, as long as you know that you're doing the best you can with the circumstances that you find yourself in, you have absolutely nothing to apologise for!

Hold your head up high, stand up for what you believe in, and stop apologising for who you are. Don't feel bad about making your mental health and happiness your priority. Don't worry about people's expectations or peer pressure. Don't worry about other people's uninvited judgement or opinions. In every situation, make sure you do what is right for you. And the only person who knows what is right for you…is YOU!

3 LIVE WHILE YOU CAN!

Carpe Diem! Seize the day! It's such a cliché, but you really do not know how many days, months or years you have left! Whilst we would all love to live for many years to come, the fact is you never know what might be around the corner. You never know when your life is going to come to an end! And so, we have no option other than to live our lives to the absolute full whilst we still can!

You know the famous quote: 'You only live once…but if you do it right, once is enough!' It is essential that we seize every single day – and yes, that includes Mondays! – as another opportunity to live our lives to the full! We need to stop holding back and stop delaying our efforts to 'live our best lives'!

There really is no time like the present! You need to seize every day and embrace every opportunity to live your best life, fulfil your potential, and thrive as an individual!

We need to live, laugh and love whilst we can! That clock is always ticking, and there is never any guarantee that tomorrow is ever going to come. As a result, we must commit to living fearlessly authentic and deeply fulfilling lives at every single moment made available to us!

Stop putting off your success, stop depriving yourself of happiness, and stop holding yourself back. Say 'YES' to that opportunity and be brave enough to take that big risk! Realise that whatever happens in your life, you can handle it! Life is too short to be spent hiding away in your comfort zone! Life is too short to be spent worrying about what other people might think!

Life is precious, and so are you. This is your one and only lifetime on this planet. That's why it is so important to seize the day, embrace every opportunity and live a fearlessly authentic life. You never know which day is going to be your last, so stop depriving yourself of happiness and success!

Take that risk, seize that moment, and start that conversation! If somebody invites you to do something or if an amazing opportunity arises, don't put it off until tomorrow!

Put yourself out there and make some amazing memories! Let go of your worries, step outside of your comfort zone, and give yourself permission to thrive!

See every day as an adventure and live your life to the full whilst you can!

4 LIVE A FEARLESSLY AUTHENTIC LIFE

Happiness in life is the result of fulfilling your potential and becoming the very best version of yourself. And the secret to fulfilling your potential as a human being is daring to live an unapologetically authentic life.

You cannot fulfil your potential and thrive if you are living a life of conformity or denial. You cannot become the best version of yourself if you are constantly pretending to be somebody else. Trying to act your way through life is utterly exhausting. To spend every second of your existence, trying to win approval or live up to expectations is seriously soul-destroying.

Martin Luther King Jr wrote about the 'modern world where everyone seems to crave the anaesthetising security of being identified with the majority'. He observed the 'crowd pressures' that have 'unconsciously conditioned our minds and feet to move to the rhythmic drumbeat of the status quo'.

In modern society, it's very easy to get lost amongst a sea of consumerism and conformity. In a world where everyone is chasing the latest trends and is desperate to look good on social media, individuality and integrity have become very disposable indeed.

Whilst conformity may bring you temporary social acceptance; this will never bring you genuine contentment or fulfilment in life. When it comes to achieving external approval or validation, you must always ask yourself this – at what cost? As the New Testament asks us, 'What good will it be for someone to gain the whole world, yet forfeit their soul? Or what can anyone give in exchange for their soul?'

Albert Einstein famously once said this: 'The one who follows the crowd will usually get no further than the crowd. The one who walks alone is likely to find themselves in places no one has ever been before'.

We know that our lives are so precious, which is why it is so important to live every single day as our most authentic and empowered selves. We must fearlessly speak our truths and unashamedly live our best lives. Remember, as long as you are not causing anybody any harm; you have absolutely nothing to apologise for. By cultivating individuality and living with authenticity, you are helping to make the world a brighter and better place.

It is only when we commit to carving out our unique path that we can make an impactful contribution to the common good of society. Through your individuality, you can bring insight and become an inspiration to others.

If you want to fulfil your potential and flourish, then you need to get serious about living an unapologetically authentic life. As John Stuart Mill wrote, 'it is only the cultivation of individuality which produces, or can produce, well-developed human beings'.

Strive to be someone of conviction, not conformity. Stand up for what you believe in and confidently speak your truth. Know your values and know your identity is valid.

As St Paul wrote in his letter to the Romans, 'Do not conform to the pattern of this world, but be transformed by a renewing of your mind' (Romans 2:12).

Breathe new life into your existence by reflecting on what it means to be unashamedly you. Fulfil your potential by following your heart, chasing your dreams, and becoming the very best version of self. In the words of Abraham Lincoln, 'whatever you are, be a good one'.

5 LIFE IS ABOUT PROGRESS NOT PERFECTION

Life is all about progress, not perfection. Contrary to how things might appear on social media, nobody on this planet has a perfect life. Behind the airbrushed pictures and Instagram filters, we are all living equally vulnerable lives. Indeed, perfectionism is nothing more than – in the words of Brene Brown – "a defensive move…it is twenty-ton shied we lug around, thinking it will protect us".

Far from protecting us, perfectionism is the biggest barrier to our happiness and flourishing in life. As Brown explains: Perfectionism is, at its core, about trying to earn approval,…perfectionism is not the key to success.

In fact, research shows that perfectionism hampers achievement. Perfectionism is correlated with depression, anxiety, addiction, and life paralysis or missed opportunities. Perfectionism is a self-destructive and addictive belief system that…sets us up to feel shame, judgment and blame, which then leads to even more shame and self-blame".

Perfectionism is not only counter-productive, but it is incredibly toxic as well. It's not only seriously unhelpful, but it is deeply harmful to you!! It is only when we break free from our obsession with perfection and our fear of failure that we can finally start living a genuinely fulfilling life.

Perfectionism is nothing more than an obsession with perception – it stems from a desire to control how other people see you, and a desperate attempt to minimise feelings of shame, judgment and blame.

But here's the thing: you have no control over how other people see you! The only thing you will ever have control over is you! And so, you need to refocus your efforts and attention. Instead of being a slave to perfectionism, see yourself as a student of the universe. Instead of worrying about how you look to other people, focus on learning and growing through everything that you experience!

Life is not about perfection; it's about progress. At the end of the day, nobody actually cares that you made a mistake or that you didn't win every race! People are too busy worrying about their own lives to care that much about yours! So stop worrying about how you look and start focusing on learning through everything that you experience in life! This is the secret to living a happy life!

Your life is all about progress! Life is all about learning and growing through everything that we go through. As we go through each day, our focus should be on self-growth and personal development. What can our experiences teach us about both ourselves and the world? How can we learn from our mistakes and grow through what we go through? What insight and inspiration can we gain from the people that we meet? How can the challenges we encounter become catalysts for our personal development?

As you go through life, make *progress* and self-development your priority. Abandon the idea that you should – or could – ever achieve perfection. Instead, resolve to keep growing and keep learning through every single situation that you encounter. See yourself as a student at the 'school of life' and remember to keep 'growing through everything that you go through'! Mistakes and setbacks are nothing to fear. You do not need to look flawless or be perfect in order to have value or worth as a human being! No matter where you are up to in life or what you look like in the mirror today, you are doing just fine.

KNOW YOUR WORTH

At all times, know your worth. In every moment, remember your value. Wherever you go, be grounded in self-confidence and self-belief. Nothing is more important in life than knowing your worth and recognising your value as a human being!

Your worth as a human being is both infinite and unconditional. No matter what happens in life, you will always have intrinsic – and unshakeable – value.

Your worth is never dependent on your appearance, success, popularity or any other superficial factor that society might use to try and measure you. Your achievements or your public approval rating do not have any influence over your worth and value as a human being.

Instead, you are valuable just because you are you. Your worth is fundamentally unconditional, meaning that it will always exist irrespective of whatever is going on in the world around you.

Whether you are living in a mansion or you are barely managing to afford food for the day, you have unconditional worth as a human being. It doesn't matter whether you are a supermodel or a supermarket assistant, a lawyer or a dog walker – every single human being is equal in their unconditional worth.

Simply because you woke up this morning, you have worth. Simply because you are alive and breathing, you have infinite value. Nothing, or nobody, can ever take that worth away. In the words of Gandhi, 'They cannot take away our self-respect if we do not give it to them'.

Remember that you do not need other people's approval or favourable assessment to have worth. Instead, your worth comes from within. It is intrinsic, infinite and unconditional. Wherever you go and whatever you do, always know your worth. You deserve happiness just as much as the next person.

And you are just as valuable as absolutely anybody else on this planet! Never forget that!

6 YOU ARE ENOUGH

You are enough - exactly as you are. You have nothing to prove, to anybody. You are valuable, you are complete, and you are simply fine as you are. Always remember that your worth as a human being is completely unconditional

Know with confidence that your value as a human being comes from within. You do not have to impress or please anybody, and you do not need to live up to anybody's expectations, to have worth as an individual. Your worth comes from within! Your value is unshakeable!

Every time that you step outside of your front door, always remember that you are enough. Hold your head up high, walk with confidence, and know your worth.

Know that you are likeable, valuable, and worthy of happiness and success. No matter what has happened to you, no matter what anybody else thinks, and no matter what you have (or don't have), you will always be enough. Your worth and value are absolutely and fundamentally unconditional.

No matter what gets done or how much is left undone, you are always enough. At all times, you are worthy of love and belonging.

In her book The Soul of Money, Lynne Twist writes this: 'We spend most of the hours and the days of our lives hearing, explaining, complaining, or worrying about what we don't have enough of…By the time we go to bed at night, our minds are racing with a litany of what we didn't get, or didn't get done, that day…This internal condition of scarcity, this mind-set of scarcity, lives at the very heard of our jealousy, our greed, our prejudice, and our arguments with life'.

You don't have to continue living with a 'never enough' mindset! There is an alternative way of living, one that is so much more fulfilling! Start living with the 'you are enough' mantra, and you will totally transform your quality of life!

Remember– no matter how many times you make a mistake, and no matter how many times people might reject you or put you down, your value will always remain the same. Your worth as a human being is strictly non-negotiable! And so, at all times, remember that you are not only enough…you are more than enough.

7 BE KIND TO YOURSELF

Be kind to yourself! Stop beating yourself up! Give yourself the compassion, understanding and acceptance that you deserve!

So many of us are far too harsh on ourselves. We criticise, berate and judge ourselves in a way that we would never consider treating other people. We let embarrassment, shame, and self-directed anger take over our lives, leaving us feeling deeply inadequate and desperately unfulfilled. By holding ourselves to unrealistically high standards and imposing on ourselves unnecessarily demanding expectations, we set ourselves up for a lifetime of unfulfillment and failure.

 By comparing our real lives to the airbrushed and stage-managed lives we see on social media, we add even more feelings of unfulfillment and inadequacy into the mix. In the end, we end up with a totally distorted self-image which becomes incredibly damaging for our self-esteem and mental wellbeing.

Well enough is enough! You've been beating yourself up, putting yourself down, and feeling like a failure for too long! You don't need to keep comparing and criticising yourself! Instead, you deserve to treat yourself with kindness, compassion and understanding!

Just ask yourself this: has all the criticising and complaining helped you? Has the self-critical approach led to happiness and success in life? No, of course, it hasn't! All it has done is left, you feeling inadequate and unfulfilled! Is that really what you deserve in life? Is that really the secret to living your best life? Louise Hay once said this: 'Remember, you have been criticising yourself for years, and it hasn't worked. Try approving of yourself and see what happens'.

Self-love is the essential foundation for living an authentic, confident and resilient life as a human being. It provides not only a secure foundation for your relationship with yourself, but it also provides the foundation for all your other relationships in life as well. As Ru Paul asks, 'If you can't love yourself, then how in the hell are you going to love anybody else?'

Indeed, the New Testament command to 'love your neighbour as yourself' is dependent on the assumption that you actually treat yourself with kindness and compassion in the first place!

So be kind to yourself! Remember that you're doing your best! Speak to yourself in the same way that you would speak to a loved one! Love your perfect imperfections and unconditionally accept who you are! Be a good friend to yourself and really make an effort to understand why you are the way that you are. Be compassionate and forgiving towards yourself. Cut yourself some slack and give yourself the space that you need.

Talk to yourself in the way you would talk to someone you love and care about. Focus on making progress, not perfection. Remind yourself that you're doing the best you can with what you have, and that is more than enough.

Most importantly, remind yourself that you are enough. Just because everything didn't work out as planned, you are not a failure. Just because you slipped up or missed out on something, your entire life is not ruined. Be kind to yourself and just remember that you are doing the very best that you can. Life is not about comparing or criticising yourself; it's about becoming the very best version of yourself.

Make time to treat yourself and make it your life's mission to unconditionally accept who you are. You have nothing to prove and nothing to explain. Instead, you are free to live a fearlessly authentic existence!

As long as you are not harming anybody, you have absolutely nothing to apologise for! So see your life as an amazing opportunity to flourish and thrive as the authentic, imperfectly perfect individual that you are!

At the end of the day, you are the one person you will be with from the moment that you are born until the day that you die. It is therefore essential that you like the person that you are. Otherwise, that lifetime is going to feel like a very long time indeed!

In the words of Pema Chodron, 'Be kinder to yourself. And then let your kindness flood the world!' Treat yourself with kindness and compassion, and then let that kindness and compassion radiate out into the world!

8 DOING GOOD DOES YOU GOOD

Doing good does you good! Helping others helps you as well! In the words of St Francis of Assisi, 'it is in giving that you will receive!'

An essential part of living a genuinely happy and fulfilling life is contributing to the common good of society. No man is an island, and no man can find genuine contentment in life on his own! We find ourselves by making meaningful contributions to the common good of society. And we enjoy success when we do something to serve the greater good of human progress, unity and evolution!

There is nothing more rewarding than making a meaningful contribution and completing random acts of kindness as you go about your daily life. Look for opportunities to be that rainbow in somebody's clouds, without expecting anything in return. Strive to be someone who inspires, motivates and supports the people around them. Do as much good as you can, as often as you can.

Wherever you go, strive to leave a positive legacy in your wake. Whatever you do, strive to make that meaningful contribution to the common good of society.

Ultimately, we should all aspire to leave the world in a better place than it was when we arrived. When we all play our small part in making this world a better place, we achieve extraordinary things!

And remember, doing good always does you good as well! Nothing nourishes your soul or enriches your life like doing good and contributing to somebody else's happiness or wellbeing, especially without expecting anything in return!

If you want to live a meaningful life, then make it your mission to do as much good as you can. Every single day, look for opportunities to support, inspire and empower other people. It is through supporting others than we thrive ourselves!

Strive to be a rainbow in someone's cloud! Aspire to inspire the people around you! Make that contribution to the common good of society and seize every opportunity to perform a random act of kindness! At all times, remember this timeless truth - doing good does you good!

9 KNOW YOUR WORTH

At all times, know your worth. In every moment, remember your value. Your worth as a human being is both infinite and unconditional. Irrespective of what anybody else might do or say, your worth can never be undermined or taken away.

Furthermore, your worth as a human being is not dependent on whether you are wealthy, popular or a winner at something – you have unconditional worth based solely on the fact that you are human! Your worth, which is intrinsic in origin and eternal in duration, does not need to be earned and it can never be taken away.

At all times, it is essential that you know your worth. If anybody tries to put you down or undermine you, don't you dare put up with it! Set high standards for how you expect to be treated by other people; do not put up with people disrespecting or mistreating you. If they cannot recognise your worth or respect you as a human being, then you do not need them in your life. Remove yourself from any relationships where you are not being treated with dignity, recognition, and respect. If anybody makes you feel worthless, they must be removed from your life immediately.

Similarly, have the self-respect to walk away from any situation that you feel is undermining or harming you as an individual. No amount of money, achievement, popularity, or so-called success is worth selling your soul or sacrificing your inner peace for. Don't do anything that drags you down or causes you harm as an individual – you're worth so much more than that! Remember: you deserve to be happy and you deserve to live your best life!

Most importantly, always remember that your worth cannot be reduced to any quantifiable measurements such as your wealth, level of popularity, or even waistline. Worth is not a comparison competition and it is not a quantifiable concept. Worth is not a conditional entity. The worth of every and every human being on this planet is unequivocal and unconditional. At all times, know your worth! Keep your head held high, be kind to yourself and command the respect that you deserve!

10 ALL OF YOUR FEELINGS ARE VALID

Every single one of your feelings are valid. Every single one of your emotions is justified. You don't have to feel bad or embarrassed about how you feel. Whatever emotions you are experiencing right now, they are valid. Whatever feelings you are experiencing right now, you can handle them. Everything is going to be okay, even if you are not okay right now.

Whatever you do, don't fight your feelings. Whatever you do, don't deny your emotions. Human beings are supposed to experience an entire rainbow of feelings and emotions. Dare to be vulnerable, safe in the knowledge that you are capable of handling every single one of your emotions.

Indeed, nothing showcases strength better than your willingness to acknowledge and observe emotions such as anger and upset. By acknowledging and accepting – rather than suppressing and denying – these feelings, we become capable of responding to them in mature and intelligent ways.

A refusal to acknowledge your emotions only serves to drive them underground, resulting in even greater pain down the line. The idea that you can just 'think positive' and ignore all of the more painful emotion is absolutely ridiculous! Every single human being on this planet experiences feelings of pain, sadness, anger, and hurt. It is normal to experience every single emotion under the sun!

The key is to remember this: you do not have to be scared of your emotions! Every single one of your feeling is valid! Acknowledging a feeling does not mean you are weak or that it is going to overwhelm you! There is space for all of your feelings, so stop fighting them and start cultivating mindful awareness of them instead.

Our emotions are not only natural and normal, but they are also crucial sources of learning and insight. As a result, every single feeling should be acknowledged and accepted. Feelings don't just come from nowhere – it's therefore important to take time to acknowledge, accept and understand them!

Strive to become an expert observer of your emotions, impartially considering where they are coming from and what they can teach you. Are they telling you that you need to change something in your life? Are they telling you that there's an unresolved trauma or trigger that's bubbling away beneath the surface?

Try to become an observer of your emotions, giving them space to emerge and exist. Remember, they are just emotions; they can't hurt you! You don't have to impulsively react to them, and you don't have to become totally consumed by them! Instead, you can simply observe and acknowledge them.

Whatever you do, don't just suppress or run away from them! Remember, you are not your emotions! Your emotions and feelings do not define or control you. Instead, they can be acknowledged, understood and worked through! And, most importantly, they can be survived!

Whatever you're feeling right now, that feeling is valid. Every single one of your feelings is valid. So stop fighting how you feel and try to be a little bit kinder to yourself instead. Strive to understand, rather than fight, how you feel. Treat yourself with compassion and make space for every single one of your emotions. Validate your feelings and make peace with where you're at in life right now. You're going to be okay.

11 EVERY DAY IS A NEW BEGINNING

Every day is a new beginning. Every morning is a new opportunity to wake up and start afresh. Whatever happened yesterday is now in the past. This is a new day and a new dawn, which means it is a completely fresh start and a brand new beginning.

As Eleanor Roosevelt once said, 'With the new day comes new strength and new thoughts'. Each new day is an opportunity to wipe the slate clean and step out into the world with a renewed sense of purpose and motivation.

When you wake up every morning, remember that possibilities of the new day ahead of you are endless! Each and every new day is filled with brand new opportunities to make memories and take chances! And, even if things don't end up going so well today, you don't need to worry…because there's always tomorrow!

Have the courage to believe that even if things don't work out one day, that doesn't mean they won't go well tomorrow. Just because everything went wrong today, that doesn't mean everything will go wrong tomorrow as well!

Indeed, whatever has happened today will be forgotten about by tomorrow! So have the courage and resilience to learn from what went wrong yesterday and see tomorrow as a brand new start.

As Mary Ann Radmacher put it: Courage doesn't always roar. Sometimes courage is the quiet voice at the end of the day saying 'I will try again tomorrow'.

See every single day as a brand new beginning. Yesterday's mistakes, errors and troubles are no longer any of your concern! Wipe the slate clean and move forwards with your existence! Take a deep breath, smile and start again!

12 STRIVE TO FULFIL YOUR POTENTIAL

The purpose of your life is to fulfil your potential and thrive as the best version of your authentic self! Remember, you were not put on this planet to just survive…you were put on this planet to thrive!

When you wake up every morning, make it your mission to fulfil your potential and flourish through the day. Strive to live in accordance with your core values and aspire to make a positive difference in the world around you.

Get serious about discovering your life's purpose and living your truth every single second of your existence.

Ancient Greek philosophers such as Aristotle used the term 'eudaimonia' to refer to the state of supreme happiness achieved through fulfilling your potential as a human being.

Over 2,000 years ago, these wise thinkers had realised that the secret to achieving true happiness in life was striving to fulfil your potential and focusing on your flourishing as an authentic individual. This individual flourishing then contributed to the flourishing and prosperity of society as a whole, because each individual was then able to make their best possible contribution to the common good of society.

Take some time to consider what it would mean for you to be 'flourishing' or 'thriving' in your life today. What would 'fulfilling your potential' look like to you? What causes and core values are you most passionate about? What pursuits, practices and purpose would bring you that supreme state of happiness in your life?

Remember that you were not just born to survive, but to thrive. You are here on this planet to fulfil your potential and become the very best version of yourself.

That means discovering your life's purpose and then making that positive difference in society! When you start living your life with this deep sense of purpose, you discover more happiness and fulfilment than you had ever realised was possible!

Here's what you need to know: Your life has purpose. Your story is important. Your dreams count—your voice matters. You were born to make an impact. Seize this moment as an opportunity to make your voice heard and get serious about making your life meaningful! Fulfil your potential and thrive through life!

Stop trying to just get through each day! Instead, get serious about fulfilling your potential and thriving through life! Seize the day and fulfil your potential...put yourself out there and live your very best life!

13 MAKE CONNECTION YOUR CURRENCY

A happy and fulfilling life is one that is filled with genuine connections and meaningful relationships. As social beings, humans require strong support networks and a feeling of closeness to others in order to feel fulfilled. No man is an island, and no man can survive completely on his own! From the very second we are born, it is essential that we form and maintain meaningful connections with other human beings in the world around us.

All human life is interrelated. As Martin Luther King said in his Christmas Eve sermon of 1967, 'we are all caught in an inescapable network of mutuality, tied to a single garment of destiny'.

He continued: 'whatever affects one directly, affects all indirectly…before you've finished breakfast in the morning, you've depended on more than half the world'. Every human life is interconnected, and every single one of us belongs to one universal human family. Beyond surface-level differences such as skin colour, sexuality or political beliefs, we are all fundamentally the same: we are all just human beings! We all share the same desire for happiness and the same wish to minimise suffering. As the late Jo Cox said in her maiden speech to the UK parliament, 'We are far more united and have far more in common than that which divides us'.

With this spirit of union and belonging in mind, make connection your key currency in life. Seize every opportunity to form genuine connections and meaningful relationships with your fellow human beings. Smile at the people you see in the street, make small talk with your colleagues at work. Treat people with respect, kindness, and compassion. Take a genuine interest in how your friends and family are doing! Make eye contact, 'check-in' with people, and show them kindness without expecting anything in return!

Nothing brings us greater happiness than forming genuine connections and meaningful relationships with other human beings! As Sir Cary Cooper, an expert in workplace psychology, recently told The Times: "Good, meaningful relationships are critical to people's happiness".

Remember that we all have more in common than we realise. At the end of the day, we are all just human beings looking to experience closeness and connection with other people!

So make that connection your key currency! Don't measure the success of your life in terms of social media likes or any other comparative value – measure the success of your life in terms of the amount of love, compassion and kindness you can spread!

Judge the fullness and success of your life of how many connections you can make! Wherever you go and whomever you meet, make that effort to connect, connect and connect!

Always remember that anything that brings us closer to other human beings – in a genuine, respectful and sincere way - is guaranteed to be good for us!

14 MEASURE YOUR LIFE IN LOVE

In 21st century society, we have so many different metrics with which we can measure the success of our lives. Some people, for example, choose to measure their success as human beings in terms of their wealth, social media followers, sexual attention or even their waistline.

Others might choose to measure their life based on how many compliments they receive on a night out or how many cars they have on the drive. I want to propose one single metric with which you should measure the success of your life: LOVE!

That's right; you should measure your life in love! Forget the wealth, the social media likes and the waistline – judge the success of your life on how much love it contains! How much love are you giving out into the world around you, and how much love are you allowing yourself to receive?

Live every single day in accordance with Jesus' Golden Rule – to love your neighbour as yourself! Make it your mission to live a life overflowing with love. Care for people, complete random acts of kindness, and radiate compassion at every opportunity…all without expecting absolutely anything in return.

Seize every opportunity to form authentic connections with the people you encounter in the world around you, treating the people you meet with the kindness and compassion every human being deserves!

Dedicate every day of your existence to supporting and loving your fellow human beings. Whom can you help today? Whom can you express appreciation for this week? What can you do to show someone they are valued and loved?

Go beyond the superficial and shallow metrics of success and throw yourself into creating an existence characterised by love. This way of living is guaranteed to enrich, illuminate, and positively transform your life! In the words of St Paul, follow the way of love… it will never let you down!

15 SEE THE BIGGER PICTURE

When it comes to dealing with life's trials and tribulations, nothing is more important than a healthy sense of perspective. Learning to pause, step back and consider the 'bigger picture' is one of the most important life skills we can ever hope to cultivate.

When we get caught up in the moment, it can be very easy to make a 'mountain out of a molehill'. One rejection can feel like the end of the world, and one mistake can leave us feeling like a complete and utter failure in life. Without maintaining a healthy sense of perspective, we spend our entire lives lurching from one supposed 'disaster' to another.

In order to stop lurching from one world-ending disaster to the next, we need to learn the art of getting some perspective. When you find yourself in a situation that seemingly threatens to overwhelm you, strive to see the bigger picture beyond your immediate experience.

 Consider the extraordinary size of the world the universe, and consider how small your current problem actually appears in comparison. Consider the length of your life and remind yourself that today's front-page news will be tomorrow's chip paper! Whatever you are going through right now will not last forever. This time next week, you will probably be wondering what on earth you were worrying about!

Shifting perspective and considering the bigger picture is essential for coping with modern life. Getting too caught up in the moment can cause serious amounts of totally unnecessary suffering!

In order to live a more balanced and stable life, it is important that we learn to step back and survey the situation from a birds-eye perspective. If this moment really going to have such a massive impact on your life? Will you still be losing sleep over this issue in 10 weeks time, never mind ten years time? In the grand scheme of things, might you actually be thankful for this experience, because it taught you an essential life lesson that would help you out in the future?

We must also take a moment to 'consider the bigger picture' when it comes to getting – or not getting – what we want in life. Whilst instant gratification may be very appealing; it cannot guarantee us long-term happiness or fulfilment. Instead, it can make us a slave to our desires and a prisoner to our impulses.

As Abraham Lincoln said, 'discipline is choosing between what you want now and what you want most'. Sometimes, it is essential for us to make short-term sacrifices for the sake of our long-term success. Sometimes, the universe does prematurely close some doors so that even better ones are able to open later down the line!

Always remember that everything will work out in the end. What feels like an earth-shattering disaster right now might be considered a very valuable life lesson later on down the line! So try to keep whatever it is you're going through in perspective.

Whatever happens in your life, always ask yourself this: 'Will this matter in a years time?' Allow this question to keep you mindful of the 'bigger picture' in life. Use this question every time you seem to be getting a little bit too caught up in what is a very trivial and temporary situation!

Get serious about considering the bigger picture and putting everything that happens into perspective. Step outside of yourself and consider the situation you're currently facing from a 'birds-eye' perspective. Consider whatever is happening within the wider context of both your life and the universe at large as well. In the grand scheme of things, is this situation really so explosive? In the grand scheme of things, is this situation really a matter of life-or-death?

Always remember that you will survive absolutely anything that happens in your life. Remember that you grow and learn through everything that you go through. So keep calm, get some perspective, and keep going. Instead of letting yourself get overwhelmed by the imminent situation, try to consider that longer-term and bigger-picture perspective!

Most importantly, remember that, in the grand scheme of things, this situation is not so bad after all. No matter what happens, you're a survivor.

Everything will work out in the end. I promise you that you are going to be okay. So try to keep calm, be kind to yourself and keep the bigger picture in mind. Most importantly, whatever you're going through right now, try to just keep on going! You are a survivor!

16 WORK WITH WHAT YOU'VE GOT

'Work with what you've got' is one of my ultimate golden rules for life. Make the most of whatever situation you find yourself in. Seize every opportunity that the universe offers to you! Instead of complaining about the fact that everything in your life isn't perfect, make it your mission to meet the universe where it is right now.

Try to accept the situation, circumstances, and conditions that you are faced with, and resolve to make the most of them to the best of your ability. Think outside the box, try doing something that scares you, look at things from another angle!

Instead of fighting against the universe, look for opportunities to thrive through it instead. Rather than resisting the reality of your situation, try to see how you might turn your circumstances to your advantage. How can you become the best version of yourself within this situation? How can you overcome the obstacles and embrace the opportunities that you are presented with?

In life, we have two options: we can complain about what we don't have, or we can do our best at working with what we've got. Instead of wasting your energy complaining, invest it in getting constructive!

Remember that the universe doesn't owe you anything, but also remember that your life isn't short of opportunities to make the most of the situations you find yourself in. So try to keep positive, try to meet the universe where it is right now, and strive to work with what you've got!

17 LEARN FROM EVERY PERSON YOU MEET

Every single person you meet has an essential life lesson to teach you. Every single person you cross paths with has something insightful and inspirational to share with you. And so, you should see every single conversation that you have as an opportunity to learn and grow as a human being.

Every person you meet knows something that you don't. Every person you meet has a unique set of life experiences and a unique field of specialist knowledge that they are probably more than happy to share with you. Take an interest in people's life stories and what they have to say!

Realise that you can learn so much just by listening to every single person that you meet in life! Realise that 'what you know is a drop, what you don't know is an ocean', and see every single conversation you have as another opportunity to expand and enhance your knowledge of humanity!

As the Dalai Lama says, 'when you talk, you are only repeating what you already know. But when you listen, you might learn something new'. Whenever you meet someone, strive to ask them thought-provoking questions and really listen to their answers. Learn from their stories, experiences and anecdotes. Pay attention to their words of wisdom and allow the knowledge they kindly share with you to enrich your life.

It is a privilege for someone to share their life story, anecdotes and experiences with you. When someone opens up and shares their life lessons with you, give them nothing but your full attention. Really listen to what they have to say, and be inspired by their words of wisdom!

Remember: one single conversation could genuinely change your life! You never know what life-changing lesson the next person you cross paths with might be able to teach you!

Remember that every single person you meet in this world has an important life lesson to teach you. At every opportunity, be open and receptive to learning and growing. Keep an open mind and keep asking interesting questions!

Make an effort to listen to people's words of wisdom. See the world as your classroom and see learning as your lifelong task. Every single interaction with every single person you meet has the potential to enrich your life and educate your mind! Never miss out on this opportunity!

18 NOTHING CHANGES UNTIL YOU DO

Are you living your best life? Are you thriving each day as the very best version of yourself? Do you go through every day feeling excited, challenged, and fulfilled? If not, then why not? What is missing in your life? Or what is causing you unnecessary amounts of stress or despair?

I'm a strong believer that nothing changes in life until you do. If you aren't happy with how things are going in your life right now, don't just blame the universe and get angry about it! Don't just sit around, feeling sorry for yourself! Instead, take responsibility for your life and do something about it!

Remember that you are not a victim of life…you are the master of your own destiny! And that means having the confidence to live life on your own terms, not at the mercy of external events or circumstances!

If you want things to be different in your life, then do something about it! Become aware of the very explicit difference between the things which you can control, and the things which you cannot. Let go of your desire to fix, control or change everyone and everything around you.

Instead, focus on cultivating success, achievement and prosperity for yourself! To quote the words of Niebuhr's famous Serenity Prayer: "God, grant me the serenity to accept the things I cannot change, the courage to change the things I can, and the wisdom to know the difference".

Stop worrying about the things you cannot change or fix, and start focusing all of your energy on doing the most with the things that you do have! Nothing changes in your life until you do – so stop complaining and start changing! Get constructive and get creative!

Become the change you wish to see in the world! Make that difference and do more of the things that will help you to become the best version of yourself!

Stop fighting against the universe and learn to start thriving in it instead!

Unconditionally accept who you are and where you are in life, and then look for ways to make the most of your time on this planet.

Get proactive about fulfilling your potential. Most importantly, make it your lifelong mission to keep growing, keep glowing and keep evolving!

19 FEEL THE FEAR...AND DO IT ANYWAY

Fear is one extraordinarily powerful emotion. It has the power to paralyse and limit even the most ambitious and confident of human beings! and whilst fear may have served our ancestors an evolutionary advantage in the past, eight appears that many of our modern fears cause us so much more harm than good.

That's why we need to take back control of our fears before they take over and control our lives. Put simply, if you don't control your faith, they will totally control you. This will lead to a life of limitation, restriction, and lack of fulfilment.

You need to stop letting your fear control your life. Whilst fair can certainly be helpful in alerting us to potentially dangerous situations; fear can also have devastating effects if we let it run wild and take over our lives. Make sure fear is serving you, the other way around! Here's the thing with fear: 99% of it is all in your head!

Of course, most fears do have some kind of 'real world' foundation. However, there is an obvious difference between a helpful sense of fear that is rational, beneficial and manageable, and an irrational and paralysing sense of fear that serves no positive purpose whatsoever.

Many of the fears which paralyse us today are completely irrational and unfounded. They serve us no positive purpose and so should play no role in our lives. Here's the good news: they don't have to!

Indeed, fear can only take over your life if you let it! And you don't have to let it! Instead of letting fear paralyse you, you can start learning to feel the fear...and then daring to do the thing that scared you so much anyway!

Instead of letting fear paralyse you, you can learn to harness it! Instead, when you're next feeling the fear, ask yourself this: what's the worst that can happen here? Is this situation going to kill me? I am 99.9% sure it is not!

You actually owe it to yourself to do more of the things that scare you! You have a duty to step outside of your comfort zone, put yourself out there, and enlarge your life! As Eleanor Roosevelt once said, 'you must do the things you think you cannot do'. Realise that limitation is all in your imagination. Wake up to the fact that you are more capable and resilient than you realise!

Safe in the knowledge that 'whatever happens, you can handle it', dare to put yourself out there!

Life is all about taking risks, seizing opportunities, and facing your fears!

Every single time you do something that scares you, your life is enlarged! Every time you face one of your fears, you become so much stronger and wiser as an individual.

Confront your fears and move beyond your comfort zone! Don't be a prisoner to perfectionism, and don't limit your life because you're scared about what could potentially go wrong. Instead, dare to feel the fear…and then do it anyway!

20 IF YOU CAN DREAM IT, YOU CAN ACHIEVE IT

Life is all about following your dreams, pursuing your passions, and becoming the very best version of yourself! Know this: you were put on this planet not only to *fulfil* your potential but to exceed it and shine brighter than you ever thought possible!

All of us have dreams, and yet so few of us have the confidence to pursue them. This is an absolute scandal, not to mention a shocking waste of potential! Here's what you need to know: you are capable of achieving all of your dreams…and more! All that you need is some self-confidence, a commitment to hard work, and a spirit of determination!

Here's a mantra that I want you to start living your life by - if you can dream it, you can achieve it! With that self-confidence, hard work and determination, you can transform every single one of your dreams into reality! T

here is absolutely no reason that you cannot achieve all of your dreams in life…and more! The only thing standing in the way of you fulfilling your dreams is your own self-limiting (and utterly irrational) belief that you can't!

That's not to say that achieving your dreams is going to be easy. But, then again, nobody promised you that life would be easy! On your journey to achieving your dreams, you are guaranteed to face countless setbacks, struggles and obstacles.

You're going to get knocked down, make mistakes and hit countless brick walls. The most important thing is that you keep your mind focused on your destination, and you keep on going!

That spirit of determination – along with a commitment to perseverance and resilience – is essential! When you truly believe in your dreams, you'll find you possess this limitless capability to keep bouncing back stronger.

And when you truly believe in your dreams, you'll realise that the old saying 'when there's a will, there's a way' could not be more true! The road might be rocky, but that doesn't mean you're never going to reach your destination. Take those setbacks in your stride and keep working towards your goals!

Life is all about dreaming big and then working hard to turn those dreams into your brand new reality!

Remember, if you can dream it, you can achieve it.

With self-confidence, hard work and determination, anything is possible!

So get serious – and fearless - about fulfilling your potential and achieving all of your dreams...and more!

21 LIFE IS TOUGH, BUT SO ARE YOU

Life is tough, but so are you. Whatever happens in life, you can handle it. Whatever obstacles you encounter, you can overcome them. Every challenge is an opportunity to grow as an individual. Every setback is just another stepping-stone towards future flourishing and success.

We all know life is not easy or plain-sailing. We all know that setbacks, struggles, and mistakes are an inevitable part of our existence. We're all familiar with the experience of failure, and we're all accustomed to experiencing some degree of suffering. But one thing we're not so good at realising and recognising is that we are survivors of all of these things, not victims!

Life may be tough, but you are tougher! Stop underestimating what you are capable of surviving! Stop hiding away in your comfort zone because you think you won't be able to cope when the going gets tough!

Instead, realise that whatever happens in life, you can handle it! As Rita Mero once said: 'The hard times you go through build character, making you a much stronger person'. With that in mind, be brave enough to take risks, seize opportunities, and put yourself out there in the world!

Whenever you feel overwhelmed by events or paralysed by fear, you've got to ask yourself the key question: what is the worst thing that can actually happen here? Am I really incapable of surviving this experience?

Remember this: whatever happens, you will be able to handle it! Whatever setbacks you face or mistakes you make, you are going to survive them! Even if everything ends up going wrong (which, by the way, is highly unlikely) the world is not going to end! You're not going to be a failure…you're just going to learn a very valuable life lesson!

Remember these words from Josel Osteen: "Hard times may have held you down, but they will not last forever. When all is said and done, you will be increased". Every single person on this planet must go through suffering and hardship. It's just an inevitable part of human existence! What matters is that you choose to face this inevitable hardship and suffering with a spirit of resilience and self-confidence! Stop underestimating yourself and realise that you are capable of handling whatever challenges, obstacles and heartbreaks the universe presents you with!

No matter what happens in life, you're going to be okay. You're not just going to survive every setback and struggle you face in life – you're going to thrive as a result of them! Remember: what doesn't kill you is guaranteed to make you stronger. So, thank your universe for sending you these all-important life lessons!

At all times, remember this: You are stronger than you think! So take those risks and dare to put yourself out there! Keep persevering and keep putting everything that happens into perspective!

Remind yourself that you are a survivor. You will get through this, no matter how tough or unbearable things might seem in this moment. Realise that you are more than capable of surviving absolutely anything that happens to you in your life.

Whatever you're going through right now, keep going! You're going to survive this, I promise you! Life may be tough, but you are tougher!

22 DON'T GET BITTER, GET BETTER

How do you handle it when someone hurts you? How do you react when someone betrays, deceives or harms you, whether intentionally or not? Some of us might react by feeling victimised, and mistakenly believe that there is something wrong with us. Some of us might get angry and resolve never to trust anybody ever again.

It is, of course, perfectly natural to feel hurt, upset, and perhaps angry. But please try not to take it personally, beat yourself up or start pushing other people away. You are not the one with the problem, and you do not deserve to carry the burden of this experience around with you for the rest of your life.

When someone has hurt you, you are of course very entitled to feel upset, angry, and negatively affected by this situation. But who benefits from this bitterness? Bitterness won't affect the person or situation that caused you the harm…the only person who pays the price for your bitterness is you! Do you want to carry this bitterness around forever? Is it fair on you to keep prolonging this pain?

Instead of carrying around this burden of bitterness, I urge you to try three things: forgive, let go, and learn. This will allow you to find freedom and get back to thriving in life, which is exactly what you deserve!

Rather than seeing yourself as a victim of this situation, try to see yourself as an empowered survivor instead. Ask yourself the key question: what can I learn from this experience? How can I become stronger as a result this?

Remember my core message: you grow through what you go through! Whilst you did not deserve or desire this ordeal, you are able to gain personal growth and worldly wisdom as a result of it! Turn that pain into an opportunity for personal growth! Life is 10% what happens to you, and 90% how you have chosen to respond. And you should choose to respond to this situation in a way that will help you to grow and thrive as a human being!

So transform those feelings of bitterness into an opportunity to get better! And so, in a way, you could almost be thankful to the universe for sending you this important life lesson…your eyes have been opened, your resilience has been demonstrated, and you've learned an essential life lesson for the future!

For the sake of your happiness and future success, don't get bitter…get better! Forgive them, because even if they don't deserve forgiveness, you deserve freedom!

As the Buddha is regularly quoted as having once said: 'Holding onto anger is like drinking poison and expecting the other person to die'. Holding onto bitterness, anger and resentment will only hurt one person – YOU! Haven't you already suffered enough? Don't you deserve freedom from what happened to you in the past?

Take back control of the situation and take responsibility for your freedom from the pain of the past! Be brave enough to accept what happened, let go of the pain, and learn from this whole experience.

Stop seeing yourself as a victim, and stop carrying that anger or resentment around with you. Instead, leave the bitterness where it belongs – in the past. Don't let what they did to continue causing you pain! Don't let them continue causing you harm and dragging you down!

Instead, strive to turn that pain into an opportunity for personal growth and self-development, and focus on living your very best life into the future.

Ultimately, we are not defined by what has happened to us, but by how we have chosen to respond.

And so I hope, for the sake of your future happiness and inner peace in life, that you choose to get better, not bitter!

23 YOU ARE THE MASTER OF YOUR DESTINY

Take responsibility for your life! Realise that you do not have to be a victim of your circumstances or a slave to other peoples opinions! Instead, you can become the master of your own destiny and the author of your entire future. You alone have the power to create the life you want!

If something is triggering or upsetting you, step away from it. If someone is belittling you or putting you down, stand up for yourself. If you are presented with an exciting opportunity, seize it with both hands. Instead of feeling like a victim and wishing that things could be different in your life, get into the mindset of a victor and start working to make change happen!

You are in complete control of everything that you do as an individual. You are completely responsible for every aspect of your existence, from the food you choose to eat to the people you choose to let into your life. You cannot outsource this autonomy to anybody else!

Instead, you've got to become fully accountable for everything you do and believe in as an individual! This means that, if you're not happy about something, you have the power to change it. And it also means that, if you want something in your life, you have the opportunity to go out and get it.

It's very easy to complain and moan about how unfair life is. It's very easy to feel sorry for yourself about how unlucky you have been. But what is all this complaining going to achieve for you? Instead of continuing to complain or feel sorry for yourself, get out there and do something constructive! Don't just complain about it, do something about it!

Realise that the shape and direction of your life are completely down to you! Roll up your sleeves, take responsibility, and get down to business! Decide what you want and get confident in your capabilities.

Remember, you are not a victim of life but the master of your own destiny! So stop outsourcing responsibility, stop attributing blame, and take full responsibility for creating your dream life! If you want something, you've got to work for it! Nothing in life is ever handed to us on a plate, and nothing in life is ever plain sailing!
Yes, some people might have things easier than you – but complaining about this isn't going to change things for you! Instead, you need to invest all of your efforts and energy into achieving your dreams and living your best life!

One of my personal heroes, the Holocaust survivor and psychotherapist Edith Eger, said this: 'To be passive is to let other people decide for you. To be aggressive is to decide for others. To be assertive is to decide for yourself'.

You need to get serious about being assertive, taking full responsibility for your own decisions, and becoming 100% accountable for your own actions! Have the confidence to be the change you wish to see in the world!

Know that the power to achieve all of your dreams – and more - is entirely within your own hands! You have the complete power to create the life you want for yourself! Remember, life is 10% what happens to you and 90% how you have chosen to respond.

Stop being a victim of life and start living each day to the full. Take ownership for your existence and live every single day on your own terms. Stop complaining and start creating. Stop waiting and start winning!

Take the steering wheel, be the author of your next chapter, and become the master of your own destiny! Look yourself in the eye and take full responsibility for your life!

Become accountable for your actions and live a fearlessly autonomous existence!

24 KNOW YOUR VALUES

The secret to living a successful and meaningful life is knowing your core values. Nothing matters more than being clear and assertive about your core values and moral principles. They bring you purpose, meaning, and unshakeable integrity. They define who you are, and they outline exactly what you're all about.

When you are confident in your core values, you are unstoppable! And when you are assertive about your moral principles, you are guaranteed to live a deeply fulfilling and extraordinarily enriching life!

What does it mean to know your values? Knowing your values means knowing what you stand for, believe in, and represent in this world.

 For example, you might believe in the importance of compassion, kindness, in the supremacy of love. Or you might believe that life should be grounded in a commitment to justice, equality, and commitment to the common good.

Living in accordance with values has been an important part of human flourishing for thousands of years. Saint Paul wrote to the early Christian communities about the essential role of faith, hope, and love. And the ancient Greeks famously believed in the four Cardinal virtues of wisdom, justice, fortitude, and temperance (in modern-day terms, these would translate into wisdom, morality, courage and moderation).

I wonder what your own core values - or, if you like, Cardinal virtues - might be? Nothing gives a better insight into who you are van your core values. They provide the foundation and framework for how you live your life as a human being in this world. They determine your outlook, actions, and the ultimate purpose behind everything that you do.

Knowing your core values provides you with certainty, confidence, and a deep sense of both identity and purpose. So take time to decide on your core values as a human being!

What do you stand for? What do you value the most? What do you think it means to live a good life?

The answers to these questions will determine your core values and, in turn, your core values will determine the purpose of your life! When you live with a commitment to your core values, you are guaranteed to live a happy, fulfilling, and deeply meaningful life.

Aspire to be someone of conviction, not conformity. Morality cannot be reduced to popular opinion or a mob mentality. You must be sure in your heart that you are living your truth and acting in accordance with your core values.

Never compromise on your core values! Allow them to infuse and invigorate every area of your life instead!

Living in accordance with our core values is the key catalyst for finding fulfilment and flourishing in life.

So what are you waiting for? Get serious about living your best, core-value infused life!

25 BE CLEAR ABOUT YOUR PRIORITIES

Getting your life in order begins with getting clear about your priorities. In order to get what you want in life, you need to know what you want! In order to make the most of your lifetime, you need to know what you get out of your time here on this planet.

Here's what you need to ask yourself: What do you want to get out of life? What is the purpose of your existence? What are the most important things to me? What matters the most in my life? What core values do I care about the most? How do I want to spend my time on this planet?

These questions help us to establish what we value the most in our lives. They enable us to become clear about our priorities, which allows us to become intelligent about how we spend our time. The answers to these questions will inform us of what we truly value and what we truly want out of life. And then, once we know our priorities, we can get the most enjoyment and fulfilment out of our time on this planet.

Remember; your time is very short and very precious! It is therefore essential that we stop wasting our precious time and energy on projects, pursuits and people who are not aligning with our core values and purpose in life! Be clear about your priorities and live your life with a renewed sense of positivity and purpose!

I'm a great believer that 'in life, you only get what you put up with'. When you get clear about your priorities, you clear out anything – and anyone – not aligning with your purpose in life. You are able to detox from the endless distractions we are surrounded by that achieve nothing but the draining of our precious energy. This leaves you with so much time and energy to invest in the things that you really care about.

It allows you to finally start doing more of the things that you care about, rather than wasting your time doing things that drain you. As a result, you are able to start living your best possible life!

Remember: this is your one and only lifetime, and you deserve to live every single day of it to the full! In order to do that, you need to live it on your terms as an authentic and autonomous individual! You need to make your happiness and flourishing your priority!

And that begins with being clear about your priorities! Consider what you want out of every situation and every relationship in your life. Establish your core values and fundamental priorities. If something isn't aligning with your values or helping you to fulfil your life's purpose, then why on earth are you wasting your time on it?

Your time, effort and energy are precious. In a world of so many demands and distractions, it is essential that we are assertive! Be committed to your core values and be clear about your priorities! Make the most of your time on this planet and don't feel bad about walking away from anything – or anyone – not enriching your life or aligning with your priorities!

Strive to know the difference between what's really important and what's really irrelevant in your life. Have the confidence to be the master of your own destiny! Have the confidence to be clear about your personal priorities...and start living your best life!

26 BE SOMEBODY WHO MAKES EVERYBODY FEEL LIKE A SOMEBODY

Wherever you go in life, make it your mission to spread positivity and good energy. Seize every opportunity to make someone's day, boost someone's self-confidence and give someone the recognition they deserve!

Jump at that chance to give someone a compliment and take pride in your power to make someone feeling amazing! In short, make it your mission in life to hype people out! Wherever you go and whoever you meet, make it your mission to leave gold dust and good energy in your wake!

We live in a society obsessed with competition and comparison. We so easily forget that there is more than enough space for everybody to succeed in this world!

We so easily forget that we are so much stronger when we come together, connect and co-operate, rather than seeing every single thing in life as a competition! Remember, our greatest achievements in life are not the things that we gain for ourselves but the difference that we make in other people's lives!

So make it your mission to empower, motivate, support and inspire as many people as you possibly can. Reach out, be kind and give people sincere compliments! If someone is feeling low, give them the support that they need and deserve. If someone seems lacking in self-confidence, make an effort to empower them! Be the rainbow in someone's cloud! Be the motivator and hype man behind someone's success!

Strive to make every single person that you meet feel a million dollars. Give them the little bit of motivation, kindness and encouragement we all need and deserve!

Never underestimate the difference that a few positive words of encouragement can make. Never underestimate the power that you have to quite literally make somebody's day!

When you make it your mission to empower the people around you, the quality of your own life is totally transformed. So instantly enrich your existence by empowering others!

Motivate, inspire, empower and hype people up at every opportunity! Spread love, radiate positivity, and become a beacon of life!

Celebrate people's successes, shower people in genuine compliments, and instil every single person you meet with confidence.

Most importantly, always remember this: never look down on someone unless you are helping them up.

Enrich your existence by making it your mission to empower and encourage others. Support and encourage every single person that you meet! Spread love and positivity! Spread kindness and compassion! Always remember the words of St Francis of Assisi: it is in giving that you will receive!

27 LOVE WILL NEVER LET YOU DOWN

Wherever you go and whatever you do, live a life illuminated by love. Seize every opportunity to radiate love and show people compassion. Show kindness, express gratitude, and seek to do good. Even in the darkest and most desperate of times, love will always prevail. If you are ever in doubt or a state of despair, make sure you administer love. It will never fail you!

In the 21st century, we can often take the word 'love' for granted. Far too many people, for example, all too easily confuse the words 'love' and lust'. It appears that, for many of us, the true meaning of the word 'love' has been devalued and even lost.

I find that the Biblical definition of agape love – defined as unconditional and selfless love, the highest kind of love known to humanity – is the most powerful way of understanding what we mean by love. Love should not be conditional, shallow, or superficial. Instead, love should fundamentally transform our lives through the power of kindness and compassion.

As St Paul wrote in his letter to the Corinthians: 'Love is patient, love is kind. It does not envy, it does not boast, it is not proud. It does not dishonour others, it is not self-seeking, it is not easily angered, it keeps no record of wrongs. Love does not delight in evil but rejoices in the truth. It always protects, always trusts, always hopes, always preserve. Love never fails'.

Make love your supreme guiding principle for life. At every opportunity, administer love. Kindness, compassion and unconditional love are the most powerful forces in this universe. Love will always triumph over hate, and kindness will always triumph over cruelty. Make your life all about love, and you will love every single second of your existence.

28 YOU ARE THE DESIGNER OF YOUR ENTIRE LIFE

Take a moment to imagine yourself as if you were an architect designing a building. In front of you is a blank sheet of paper. In your hand is a freshly sharpened pencil. You must decide, from scratch, how this new building will look. You have complete artistic control and the total freedom to design whatever property you would like. Will it have a modern and contemporary feel? How will you design the windows? What colours will you choose?

Let's try to apply this architectural analogy to the design of your own life. In the same way that the architect is responsible for designing the home from scratch, you are responsible for designing the shape and direction of your entire life.

You are the architect of your own existence! The famous existentialist philosopher John Paul Sartre once said that 'man is nothing except what he makes of himself'. That's right; it is down to you to actively ***make and construct*** the life you dream of living! Remember that you are not in the passenger seat of your life – you are the driving seat, and that means you have full control over the direction your life takes!

That includes absolutely everything about your life, from the people you surround yourself with right through to the food you decide to put into your body. Everything is in your own hands! You get to decide where you spend your time, what you do with your time, and whom you spend your time with!

The prospect of having to design your life can at first seem very daunting. And I'm certainly not denying that it's a lot of responsibility! But here's the question: would you prefer to live life as the master of your own destiny or as a little snowflake at the mercy of the world around you? Would you prefer to just pray for the universe to bring you success, or work hard to achieve that success for yourself?

Designing your life is just as much about the journey as the destination! The process of dreaming big and working hard is just as rewarding as the end results (achieving your dreams in life!) Strive to enjoy the journey and start to find deep fulfilment in every moment of your existence!

So, what are you waiting for? Get our your design sketchbook and start planning out your life!

Ask yourself this: where do you want to go? Whom do you want to be? What do you want to achieve? Get serious about creating goals and outlining your ambitions! The first step in designing your life is deciding on your core values. What are your beliefs about the meaning of existence? What are the moral principles that govern everything that you do?

Decide what direction you want your life to take and then get serious about designing your life! Remember, the world is your oyster – you can do absolutely anything, go absolutely anywhere, and be absolutely anyone you want!

Sharpen your pencil, decide on how you want to spend your existence, and get busy designing! The pencil – and the power – is entirely within your own very hands!

29 IF YOU WOULDN'T TAKE THEIR ADVICE, DON'T LISTEN TO THEIR CRITICISM

Do not let the opinions of unintelligent, ignorant, rude, and nasty little people get you down. I strongly believe that whilst everybody is entitled to have an opinion about you, under no circumstances do you ever have to pay any attention to this opinion!

When it comes to deciding whether to take what someone thinks about you to heart, you should ask yourself these important questions: - Would you turn to these people for life advice or guidance? - Would you trust their opinions on your relationship dilemmas or how to overcome the challenges you were facing in your daily life? - Would you seek out their advice on how to live a good life and become the best version of yourself?

This is my strong belief: If you would not trust their advice, then DO NOT listen to their criticisms! Would you take lessons in loyalty from a serial adulterer? Would you take medical advice about a heart condition from a plumber? Would you take a lesson in quantum physics or the epistemology of religious philosophy from a two-year-old?

No, of course you would not! So why are you listening to the opinions of people who have absolutely no authority on the subject of your life? Do these people even know, care about you or have any genuine interest in you? Are they even forming an opinion about YOU or are they just saying something about the tiny aspect of your identity that they have seen?

If you would not seek out their advice, then you should never care about their opinion. If you would not seek out their wisdom, then never even consider listening to their criticisms! If you're going to listen to an opinion, then make sure it is coming from an expert!

It is so important to know whose opinions you truly value in life – and listen to these people alone.

This should begin, of course, with your own opinion and how you genuinely feel about yourself. Do you feel that you are living per your values? Do you make yourself proud and believe that you are fulfilling your potential as a human being? Then ask yourself this: Who can offer you genuinely helpful constructive criticism in your life? Who has an important role to play in your life? Who inspires you and guides you? Who genuinely cares for you and wants you to be happy? Who provides you with unconditional acceptance and love? Who has your best interests at heart?

Only those people who you would include in your inner circle have an opinion that is worth listening to. That's because it is only these individuals who can be seen as the 'experts' on you – they are the people who know you, love you and want the best for you.

Remember, every single person is entitled to form an opinion on the tiny bit of you that they see. It's human nature to make hundreds of split-second judgments and assumptions every single day. Human beings are social animals, and so it is only natural for us all to be observing, judging and evaluating the actions of other people.

You cannot complain about the fact that people have opinions about you! But you also cannot start taking other people's opinions to heart! You cannot live your life at the mercy of other people's opinions of you! Realise that the opinions that people form about us are rarely ever accurate. They should, therefore, never become our sole source of validation in life. Remember, you should only ever listen to an opinion if it is constructive criticism given to you by an 'expert' (e.g. someone you like, admire, trust and respect)!

What other people think of you is none of your business and none of your concern! They are judging a version of you that they have seen in the street, not the real you. Focus on what you think of yourself and on becoming the very best version of yourself. Only take criticism if it is constructive and it is coming from someone who you would turn to for advice.

Remember: most people's judgments of you say more about them than they say about the real you. You cannot live a life dependent on people making favourable judgements about you. It is a recipe for disaster and a guaranteed source of endless suffering and discontent.

Stop trying to be liked by everyone else and start focusing on learning to like yourself instead. Live your life following your values, not at the mercy of other people's uninformed opinions. Take back control, get those earplugs out, and stop taking other people's opinions to heart.

It is, of course, essential that we can take on board the constructive criticism many people offer to us. Indeed, whilst you should never listen to nasty comments and petty remarks, you must always be receptive to constructive criticism from people that you like, trust and admire.

Other people can advise you, but they should never be given the power to control or change you. Make sure you assess their intentions and work out whether they have your best interests at heart - if they aren't trying to help you, then don't pay them any notice whatsoever!

At all times, says Mill, your 'individual spontaneity is entitled to free exercise'. Remember this at all times! You have freedom and autonomy! You do not have to become a slave to people's opinions about you! People have a right to make whatever judgements about you they like, but you have an equal right to ignore them! As long as you are not harming anybody else, you are free to do whatever leaves you feeling truly happy and fulfilled!

Other people are more than entitled to advise you, make suggestions about things that you are doing, or offer constructive criticism. But it is you alone who is completely responsible for the choices that you make and for how you live your life.

Remember at all times that what other people think of you is none of your business! Stop paying attention to random people's unsolicited opinions! Stop craving validation or approval from irrelevant outsiders! Never forget my golden rule: Never take criticism from somebody who you wouldn't turn to for advice!

(This is an extract from 'Live Your Best Life: Essays on Authenticity, Confidence and Resilience' – available now at www.benwardle.org/shop).

30 CONNECT TO A CAUSE

What is the purpose behind your existence? What is it that makes your life meaningful? I very strongly believe that the secret to living with a sense of purpose is connecting to a cause greater than yourself.

When you commit yourself to a cause, you enrich your life with a brand new sense of meaning. Connecting to a cause enables you to step outside of yourself and make a meaningful contribution to the common good of humanity. There is nothing more enriching, empowering, or rewarding!

It's so important to discover what causes, issues, and projects you are most passionate about. Once you have discovered these important sources of interest, it is essential you make time to invest in them! Ask yourself how you can use your talents and time to make a positive difference in the world at large. What cause will you dedicate yourself to? What vision will you choose to believe in? What project will you get passionate about?

As religion has been demonstrating for over 2000 years, human beings find great fulfilment through connecting to a cause, calling or purpose greater than themselves. It enriches our souls and enlarges our lives.

When we commit ourselves to a cause, we give our lives a greater purpose and - as a result - we discover a profound source of happiness and fulfilment.

Discover the projects you are passionate about, reflect on the contribution you can make to the greater good of society, and connect to a cause that will bring purpose and fulfilment into your life. Get serious about connecting to a cause and making a meaningful contribution to the common good of society!

31 NEVER GIVE UP

Whatever you're going through, keep going. Life may be tough, but you are tougher! With grit, perseverance, and determination, you can endure every obstacle, and you can overcome every obstacle. When the going gets tough... keep on going!

Spryte Lorriano is quoted as saying that 'every great story has happened when someone decided not to give up'. If you want to succeed, you've got to be in it for the long haul! If you want to get to the top, then you've got to put in the hard work it takes to get there!

According to Malcolm Gladwell, it takes 10,000 hours of practice at something in order to become an expert. As he writes, 'ten thousand hours is the magic number of greatness'.

In other words, if you want to enjoy success in life, then you've got to work for it! At the end of the day, success in life is all about resilience and perseverance! As Arnold Schwarzenegger put it: 'Strength does not come from winning. Your struggles develop your Strength. When you go through hardships and decide not to surrender, that is Strength!'

Although modern reality TV shows and social media might promote the idea of becoming an 'overnight star', the truth is that overnight success has actually been at least ten years in the making. What you see on TV or social media is only ever 1% of the story – what they don't have time to show you on primetime Saturday night is the years of blood, sweat and tears someone has put into honing their craft or rehearsing their act!

Whilst we might dream of becoming an overnight sensation, this kind of success is not only unsustainable, but it is also deeply unfulfilling! Remember, the process is just as important as the final product! As Angela Duckworth says, 'consistency of effort over the long run is everything'.

JK Rowling – now a billionaire author – was rejected over ten times before her Harry Potter books were finally accepted by a publisher. Imagine if she had given up after her first rejection? And imagine if she had given up after her tenth rejection? The world would never have been introduced to the world of Hogwarts and wizarding, and JK would never have become the international sensation that she is today! It just shows: you cannot take setbacks or rejection personally. Just because one person doesn't like you or your idea, that doesn't mean nobody else will! And so, as the old proverb says, 'fall down seven times, stand up eight!'

If you want to achieve success and fulfil your dreams, you've got to get some grit and practice some perseverance! The secret to unlocking this perseverance is believing in the purpose behind what you're doing. As John Wayne once said: 'True grit is making a decision and standing by it, doing what must be done. No moral man can have peace of mind if he leaves undone what he knows he should have done'.

Woodrow Wilson put it like this: 'The difference between a strong man and a weak man is that the former does not give up after defeat'. Of course, it is important to know when it's time to bow out gracefully. Susan David calls this the 'Grit versus Quit' question and warns us against being so rigid and inflexible that we fail to know when it's time to throw in the towel.

She writes: 'Many people invest years pursuing unsatisfying or unrealistic choices because their afraid to admit their error...and by the time reality forces them to change course, other ships have sailed'. She continues: 'We should be gritty, yes, but not stupid'. In other words, you need to have the self-knowledge and self-awareness to know when something is worth fighting for, and when it's time for you to walk away.

If you do decide that you're doing something worth fighting for – and you'll feel that conviction deep within your soul - then you've got to throw yourself into it with every ounce of grit that you've got! Believe in the purpose behind what you're doing and relentlessly practice perseverance! Keep picking yourself up and keep reminding yourself of the importance and meaning behind your goals!

Approach life's challenges and opportunities with a spirit of grit and refuse to give up! Remember that what you're doing is too important, rewarding and fulfilling for you to fail! As Winston Churchill famously said, 'If you're going through hell...keep going!' Believe in your cause, keep going and keep growing. If you just keep powering through and taking things one day at a time, I promise you that you will get there! You've got this!

32 TREAT OTHERS THE WAY YOU WANT TO BE TREATED

In the New Testament, Jesus famously teaches his followers to 'do to others what you would have them do to you' (Matthew 7:12). Put simply; you should treat others the way you want to be treated yourself! I think that this golden rule all boils down to one word: respect. We must treat every single person we meet with respect, acknowledging each person's basic dignity and value as a human being.

Whenever you are engaging with other human beings, it is essential that you treat them with respect. As Immanuel Kant said, 'always remember that human individuals are ends, and do not use them as your means to an end'. It is never acceptable to use or objectify human beings for the fulfilment of your own needs, wishes or desires.

People don't exist to satisfy your selfish needs and desires. And people should never – under any circumstances – be manipulated, objectified, used, or exploited. Every human you meet has feelings and emotions just like you do!

Every human being is a valued and precious individual, just like you! Never look down on anybody unless you are helping them up! Never treat somebody in a way that you wouldn't mind being treated yourself!

How would you feel if someone objectified, manipulated or exploited you? Remember, you must 'do to others what you would have them do to you'. And that means treating every single person you meet with the respect and dignity that they deserve as a human being. Neve

Whenever you approach people, always remember their value and dignity as human beings. Always treat them with the respect that you would yourself want to be treated with.

If you wouldn't want someone to do something to you, then don't even think about doing it to someone else! Before you act, you must always ask: 'How would I feel if someone did this to me?' Because here's the thing – if you don't treat people with respect, then they won't treat you with respect either!

The way you treat other people has a funny way of coming straight back around to you! Karma is a force to be reckoned with! The only way to guarantee yourself good karma is treating every single person you meet with kindness and respect! Wherever you go and however important you become in life, always acknowledge the dignity and value of every single human being that you meet.

At the end of the day, we are all one humanity, and we all share the same capacity for both happiness and pain.

In all of your interactions with your fellow human beings, keep the golden rule at the forefront of your mind. Only treat others in a way that you would want to be treated yourself! Treat every single person you meet with respect, kindness and compassion! When you live in accordance with this principle, you can't go far wrong!

33 WHEN LIFE GIVES YOU LEMONS, MAKE LEMONADE

Life is never plain sailing. Things rarely work out as planned. Just take a look at the Coronavirus pandemic of 2020 – one minute you were going about your daily life, as usual, the next minute the world had quite literally been shut down! As the old Yiddish proverb says, 'we plan, God, laughs'.

Things rarely work out as we have planned, but that's okay. What matters is not whether things go perfectly plan, but how you respond, adapt, and evolve when they don't! Indeed, the secret to success in life is being able to evolve and adapt to whatever situation you find yourself in! Remember – life is 10% what happens to us and 90% how we choose to respond! To quote a popular aphorism, 'Things work out for the best for those who make the best out of how things work'.

Indeed, it is only when our plans go 'wrong' that wonderful, unforeseen things are allowed to occur! Sometimes, what appears to be the biggest obstacle in life is actually our greatest opportunities in disguise! Martin Luther King Jr once said this: 'the ultimate measure of a man is not where he stands in moments of comfort or convenience, but where he stands in times of challenge and controversy'. When you are challenged, *that* is your time to shine!

Where would we be today without the tough times and challenges that we have been through in the past? Do you think you would be where you are today if everything in the past had worked out as planned?

Some of our greatest opportunities in life arise as a result of adversity! Our biggest setbacks are often the best stepping stones towards success! Sometimes, one door must close so that an even better one can be opened! As Chuck Swindell put it: 'We are all faced with a series of opportunities brilliantly disguised as impossible situations'.

If your plans happen to fall apart, see this as an opportunity to turn a setback into success! Remember: the secret to success in life is being able to evolve and adapt to whatever situation you find yourself in!

This is your opportunity to make something amazing happen! Seize this chance to adapt, diversify, divert and rethink your approach! Stop fighting against reality and figure out how you can make a success of your situation instead! Remember, whatever happens, you can handle it. And whatever happens, you can make a success of it!

Shane Koyczan puts it like this: 'If your heart is broken, make art with the pieces'. Make it your mission to adapt to your circumstances and make the most of what you've got! Turn adversity into opportunity and see setbacks as a stepping stone towards success! Just because your original plan has all gone wrong, that doesn't mean you are now incapable of ever reaching your destination.

Pick yourself up, dust yourself off, and start thinking outside the box! Get fearless about adapting and evolving! Stop fighting the situation and look for opportunities to thrive because of it instead!

Work with what you've got and make the best out of every situation you find yourself in! Be confident and get creative! When life gives you lemons, make lemonade!

34 MAKE PEACE WITH YOUR PAST

Your past does not define you. Whatever you have done – or whatever someone has done to you – does not dictate who you are or what you do today. You do not deserve to be a prisoner to your past.

Remember that whatever has happened in your past was a life lesson, not a life sentence. Have the confidence to make peace with your past and then let it go. If it's something that you did, take responsibility for it and forgive yourself. If it's something that someone else did to you, resolve to realise that you are not to blame and forgive the situation. Give yourself time, space, compassion and understanding. Open your heart and soul to receiving peace, rehabilitation and healing. Grant yourself freedom for the future.

Instead of dwelling on what might have happened in the past, focus on whatever it is you are doing today. Be thankful for the fact that you are alive, and try to anchor yourself in each breath you breathe today. Remember what Eckhart Tolle teaches us: 'the present moment is all that you ever have'.

The past is a place of reference, not residence. It cannot be changed, erased or replaced – it can only be accepted. The world has moved on from whatever happened…the question is, have you? Stop punishing yourself and stop holding yourself hostage to the past. Strive to learn a life lesson from the experience and then let it go.

At all times, remember that you are the master of your own destiny and author of your next chapter! Be kind to yourself and open your heart to healing! Leave the past where it belongs – in the past! You are not a prisoner or a victim to your past – you are a survivor and the master of your future!

Here's what you need to know: your past does not define you. Whatever has happened, happened. There's no point continuously beating yourself up or putting yourself down because of it! Try and look for the lesson and let it go! Move on with your life! Be thankful for the life lesson! Make peace with the situation and let yourself be free!

In her extraordinarily inspiring book 'The Choice', Edith Eger talks about the importance of making peace with your past. Here's what she writes: 'Here you are! In the sacred present. I can't heal you – or anyone – but I can celebrate the choice to dismantle the prison in your mind, brick by brick. You can't change what happened; you can't change what you did or what was done to you. But you can choose how you live now. My precious, you can choose to be free'.

You do not have to be defined by your history. You do not continue punishing yourself or paying the price for what happened in your past. Instead, you can choose to be free. Are you brave enough and bold enough to make that choice and liberate yourself from your self-imposed suffering?

Your past does not define you, and your past does not have to continue causing you pain in the present or the future. If people cannot see beyond your past, then they don't deserve a place in either your present or your future.

Mike Dikta puts it like this: 'I don't believe in living in the past. Living in the past is for cowards. If you live in the past, you die in the past'.

Only surround yourself with people who accept and see you for who you are today. If they cannot look beyond your past, why on earth do they have any airtime or influence over your present? Don't dwell on the past of a person who is trying to improve their future! Whilst life can only be **understood** backwards, it can only be **lived** forwards.

Let us return to one last piece of wisdom from Dr Eger, who reminds us that we all have a choice over how we choose to live our lives. She writes this: 'You can live to avenge the past, or you can live to enrich the present'.

Make peace with your past and let go of everything that has happened. Consciously choose to live life in the present and look forwards to the future!

Your past does not define you! So make peace with everything that you have been through, and look forwards to a brighter tomorrow! Learn from your past experiences, and then leave them where they belong…in the past!

35 DARE TO BE VULNERABLE

Andre Berthiaume once made this rather philosophical observation: 'We all wear masks, and the time comes when we cannot remove them without removing some of our own skin'. In order to cope with the pressures and challenges of life in modern society, we all create masks and construct social façades.

These masks provide us with a sense of security and stability when it comes to existing and interacting in the social world. They give us something to hide behind and take refuge in when we are anxious about being judged, scared of being rejected, or struggling with insecurities.

Love has a powerful way of removing the mask we insist on wearing. When we feel safe, secure and unconditionally accepted, we finally the confidence to remove the mask we have been wearing all our lives. When we feel surrounded by a bubble of love and acceptance, we dare to 'drop-down our guard' and reveal our 'true selves' to a select few of our fellow human beings.

Dropping our masks and revealing our true selves is essential for the development of close relationships and meaningful connections. In order to experience depth and connection in our relationships, we have to dare to be vulnerable.

Here's what I know for sure: you cannot form a meaningful friendship with someone who is constantly hiding behind a façade! You cannot enjoy a genuine relationship with someone who is refusing to let you in beyond the impenetrable walls they have been constructing their entire lives.

Here's what you need to ask about the friends, family members and lovers in your life today: do these people love the authentic you or do they love the mask that you put on every day? Have you given these people the chance to meet the vulnerable, flawed and very human individual behind your socially constructed façade? Or are you continuing to take refuge behind the mask and walls you have constructed around you?

Psychologists use the metaphor of an onion to describe the 'social penetration theory' of relationships. According to this theory, relationships develop as communication between the individual's involved moves from relatively shallow topics to deeper, more intimate discussions. This reciprocal exchange of information – increasing in breadth and depth – brings the two individuals closer together. According to this approach, we all have a public image, which is the outer layer of a person that is visible to many others. In contrast, the private self is the innermost layers of a person that are only revealed to significant others over time through disclosure.

So, for example, when we first meet someone, we will only reveal 'surface-level' information and make 'small-talk' about topics such as the weather. But, as we build up trust and develop our relationship with this individual, we have the confidence to reveal more about our religious convictions, deeply held fears, biggest dreams, and authentic self.

The secret to strengthening our relationships – and so achieving greater fulfilment in our lives – is daring to be vulnerable and reveal ourselves as flawed, imperfect beings.

This does, of course, come with the risk of rejection, something guaranteed to trigger feelings of anxiety and fear. But what would you prefer? A superficial life of surface-level and artificial relationships, or a meaningful life comprised of authentic, raw, and real relationships? If we do not take risks in life, we cannot flourish or thrive as individuals! Just remember this: even if somebody does end up rejecting you, it is not the end of the world. You will survive!

If you want to live a genuinely meaningful existence, you need to get comfortable with daring to be vulnerable! We need to take off our masks and dare to reveal our authentic and flawed selves to the people closest to us.

As Brene Brown writes, 'vulnerability is not winning or losing. It's having the courage to show up when you can't control the outcome'. It means revealing whom you are and daring to wear your heart on your sleeve, and stepping out from behind your carefully constructed public image. It means dropping your guard, opening up and

As Brene Brown writes, 'You are imperfect, you are wired for struggle, but you are worthy of love and belonging'.

Let the people you love and trust in. Dare to let your carefully constructed mask slip. Have the courage to show up and be seen. Here's how I see it: vulnerability may be difficult, but vulnerability is a risk that we have to take if we want to experience genuine connection in our lives.

So invest time, effort and energy into building secure relationships within which you can dare to be vulnerable. Commit yourself to building relationships anchored in unconditional love, acceptance and understanding.

Find the courage to show up and let your authentic self be seen. Prioritise these secure and meaningful relationships. They may take a lot of time and investment – and they may come with a certain degree of risk – but they totally enrich our worldly lives.

Dare to let down your guard, let your trusted loved ones in and wear your heart on your sleeve. Dare to be vulnerable!

36 STOP COMPARING AND START CREATING

Envy is the ugliest of human emotions. As Shakespeare wrote in his famous play Othello, ' jealousy is the green-eyed monster which doth mocks the meat it feeds on'.

Constantly comparing yourself to others is a recipe for self-hatred and deep unhappiness in life. There is absolutely nothing to be gained from constantly comparing yourself to others. Instead of comparing yourself to others, get busy creating a successful life for yourself. Instead of envying other people's achievements, congratulate them on their success ... And commit to working hard to achieving your own. Just because someone else has succeeded, it doesn't mean you can't as well. Indeed you should strive to turn envy into inspiration, and know that if they can achieve so much success... then so can you!

 So be genuinely happy for them, congratulate them, and see their success as a positive source of inspiration! Remember, if they can achieve it, then so can you! There's room for everyone to succeed in this world! But you will never get the chance to succeed if you're too busy being bitter about other people's success!

Think about it: how can you create a successful life if you're too busy being consumed by envy for other people? You can't! If you really want success, stop envying other people's lives and work hard to make a success of your own! There's room for everybody to succeed in this world, but you're never going to succeed if you're too busy feeling bitter about other people's achievements!

Envy won't only stop you from enjoying success, but it will also destroy your soul. Envy is the ugliest, most unproductive and poisonous of human emotions.

It will destroy friendships, happiness and inner peace. Don't you dare put up with it! Don't you dare let yourself become that bitter, negative, and deeply jealous person. It will scare people away from you and stop you from ever finding true success or happiness in your life! I am a great believer that the root cause of envy is insecurity. Indeed, your experience of envy says so much more about you than the person it is supposedly directed towards. In other words, don't take your insecurities out on them!

Whenever you catch yourself becoming consumed by envy, try to calmly ask yourself why you don't feel fulfilled in your own life. What is triggering your envy? What is fuelling your jealousy?

Work out what you really want from your life, and what will bring you genuine happiness, content and fulfilment in your own existence! Once you've discovered what you want from life, get busy working to achieve it! Be so busy achieving your dreams that you don't have any time – or any need – for comparison with or envy of other people!

Here's what I promise you: when you're finally secure and working towards achieving meaningful success in your own life, you'll find that envy is no longer dominating and ruining your life!

Stop comparing and start creating. Stop wasting your energy feeling bitter about other people's successes and get busy creating your own! Find security and fulfilment within your own skin, and you'll stop being so bitter about other people's good fortune! Don't measure your worth or success in comparison to the achievements of others.

Instead, remember that the only person you should ever compete with is who you were yesterday. Get busy growing, glowing and thriving through your life! In the words of an old aphorism: a flower does not think of competing with the flower next to it…it just blooms.

Release yourself from the prison that is envy and start flourishing in your own life!

37 NEVER JUDGE A BOOK BY IT'S COVER

Human beings love to put one another in (metaphorical) boxes. There's something that mankind just absolutely loves about labelling. We take one glance at people and categorise them. Society doesn't think twice before putting people into boxes and then never letting them escape. As a result, we have a very one-dimensional approach to understanding other people, based solely on stereotypes, first impressions, and surface-level appearances.

Do not let these stereotypes and first impressions define you! And do not let labels and assumptions influence how you perceive other people! Do not spend your life living in accordance with societally-imposed boxes! Remember that you are a human being, not a stereotype! There's so much more to you than other people's first impression!

Here's how I see it: if people cannot look beyond first impressions or physical appearance, then that is their problem, not yours! You are not defined – in any way, shape or form – by the box society has placed you into! You are more than capable of being and doing whatever you want in life, irrespective of whatever labels society has put on your head!

Being underestimated can actually be a massive advantage. Being the underdog comes with an extraordinary number of benefits! Without the pressure of expectation, you can get ahead and thrive! Whilst society is underestimating you; you can be busy working hard and getting ahead!

Remember: if people don't realise just how amazing and intelligent you really are, then that is their loss and not yours! Let them delude and deceive themselves! Let them live their life as a slave to stereotypes and assumptions!

When you a free from the pressure of social expectation, you can work hard to achieve and enjoy success for yourself, not because you need to live up to society's expectations for you! Live your life in accordance with your core values, not what you think society expects from you!

Rise above other people's assumptions about you. Don't let societally imposed labels limit you! You were not born to be put in a box; you were born to thrive as an authentic and autonomous individual! You do not have to be defined by anybody else's assumptions, prejudices, or labels. You are a human being, not a stereotype!

There's more to you than what people assume when they first look at you! If you can, turn people's stereotypes and assumptions to your advantage. Play up to them when it serves you but refuse to ever let them limit or restrict you! Always remember that you never owe anybody an explanation, and never forget that there's more to you than a socially-imposed label.

In the same way, we must always try to look beyond labels and assumptions whenever we meet new people. Try to see the people you meet as human beings, not stereotypes. Take your first impressions into account, but don't put people into inescapable boxes as a result of them.

Give people a chance to reveal themselves to you, rather than making assumptions, jumping to conclusions, and defining them by your first impressions! Make an effort to understand the people you meet, rather than just making assumptions about them. As the popular aphorism goes, never judge a book by its cover!

Here's how I see it: as long as human beings exist, stereotypes and labelling will remain. The trick is to remember that these labels and assumptions do not define you! There is more to you than a stranger's first impression! Focus on living a fearlessly authentic life as the three-dimensional human being that you are!

Look beyond the limitations of labels and stop defining people by first impressions! Take a more holistic approach to the people you meet by considering them as human beings rather than stereotypes!

Never judge a book by its cover and underestimate people at your peril! Refuse to be defined by stereotypes and never feel boxed in by other people's labels. Accept yourself and accept every single person that you meet. Live with an open mind and a commitment to authenticity. Make an effort to read the book, rather than just judging it by it's cover!

38 YOU GROW THROUGH WHAT YOU GO THROUGH

This has to be one of my all-time favourite – if not number one favourite! - mantras! It's a mantra that really gets to the heart of what it means to be a human being! As you know, I believe that life is all about progress, not perfection. And the best way of making progress in life is by committing to keep growing through what you go through!

As Arnold Schwarzenegger put it: 'Strength does not come from winning. Your struggles develop your strength. When you go through hardships and decide not to surrender, that is strength!'

Every single experience, and every single individual, has something important to teach us. Everywhere we go, there is an important life lesson to learn! The old saying 'you learn something new everyday' could not be more true!

Whatever happens in your life, you can learn from it. Whether you've made a mistake or achieved success, you can learn something from every single experience. And this practice of learning from our experiences – and so growing through what we go through – is the secret to living your best ever life!

Whatever happens in your life, I urge you to look for a lesson behind it. Someone might reject you, a project might not work out, you might miss out on an opportunity, or you might make a massive mistake.

Or, you might win a competition, have a really successful first date, get the exam results of your dreams, or make millions from your new business venture. Whatever happens, don't obsess about the outcomes…instead, pay attention to the lessons!

As Oprah once put it: 'Turn your wounds into wisdom'. Without struggle, there is no progress! When something difficult happens, just ask yourself this: what can I learn from this experience? What does this teach me about people, the world and who I am as an individual? How can this experience give me greater confidence, wisdom and insight for the future?

Whatever happens – good or bad – there is always a lesson to learn. Every single experience has something important to teach us! Wherever you go and whomever you meet, look for the lesson you can learn!

See yourself as a student at the school—of life and commit yourself to a lifetime of self-discovery and personal-development! Life is all about accumulating lessons, not possessions! As Dieter F Uchtdorf once said, 'It's your reaction to adversity, not adversity itself that determines how your life's story will develop'.

Grow through everything that you go through and allow every situation to help you develop as a human being! Life, after all, is about progress and not perfection!

Keep putting yourself out there and learning from life! Live your life with a 'growth mindset', and seize every opportunity the universe gives you for self-development!

Your enrolment to the school of life starts now, and lasts forever! At all times remember this: you go through what you go through! Go keep going and keep growing!

39 BE PRESENT IN THE PRESENT

How often are you actually present in the present? Of the twenty-four hours in your day, how many of them are spent with conscious awareness of the moment you are in? In our busy 21ˢᵗ century lives, so many of us struggle to just be present in the present. Instead of living in the moment, we find ourselves constantly scrolling through social media, drowning in to-do lists, and racking up ridiculous amounts of screen time. It seems that many of us spend more time staring at our phones than we spend just being present in the present moment!

This is a great shame because the present moment is the only place where we can find the greatest amount of happiness and fulfilment in our lives! It is the only place when we can fully experience the richness of human existence and enjoy a genuine feeling of flourishing.

At the end of the day, the present moment is all you will ever have. Yesterday has already gone, and there is no guarantee that tomorrow is going to arrive. Subsequently, you cannot dwell on the past or worry about the future. Instead, you must concentrate your mind on the present moment.

Over 2,000 years ago, Buddhism gave birth to a practice popularly known as 'mindfulness', which refers to the 'mental state achieved by focusing on one's awareness of the present moment, while calming acknowledging and accepting one's feelings, thoughts, and bodily sensations'. The Buddha himself is often quoted as teaching this: 'Life can only take place in the present. If we lose the present moment, we lose life'.

In order to achieve true happiness and deep fulfilment, we must open our hearts and minds to the gift of the present moment. We must make it our mission to fully immerse ourselves in the world around us, taking pride in our connection with the present.

Make it your task to fully experience every single experience you have in life. See the world through your own eyes, not through the screen of a smartphone. Focus your mind on the present moment before you, rather than on your regrets from the past or your worries for the future.

At the end of the day, the present moment is all we have, and the present moment is all we need. So arrive at this present moment, and fully appreciate everything it provides you with.

Just for a moment, stop worrying and stop scrolling. Just for a moment, be present in the present. By doing so, you will unlock your potential and discover true happiness deep within your soul.

40 REMEMBER THAT THE STORM WILL PASS

Everything in life is impermeant. No matter how final or serious things might seem right now, nothing ever lasts forever. What feels like the end-of-the-world right now will probably all be forgotten about next week. Try not to lose sight of the bigger picture. Instead of getting too caught up in the emotions of the moment, try to maintain a healthy sense of perspective. See things in their wider context and take into account the grand scheme of your life.

Tackle every challenge and situation that you face with as much dignity and resilience as you can. Keep your head held high, hold your nerve, and do what you can with what you have. Always keep in the back of your mind that this current storm will pass. Whatever is happening now will not last forever. No matter how tough things seem right now, you will survive this experience.

Rather than feeling defeated by your circumstances, try to focus on making the best of them. Stay true to your core values and conduct yourself with integrity. Keep that bigger picture in mind and keep reminding yourself that this ordeal will not last forever.

When you're in the eye of the storm, it's easy to feel like it's the end of the world. But just try to keep the bigger picture in the back of your mind. Keep reminding yourself of what's really important in your life and remain confident that you will survive this experience (because you will!)

Stay calm, stay strong, and keep thinking long-term. No matter how bad things seem right now, this storm will pass. So keep going and keep growing! You've got this!

41 EMBRACE CHANGE

In Science lessons at school, we learn all about the importance of 'adaptation'. According to the textbooks, being able to adapt was the secret to a species gaining an evolutionary advantage.

Put simply; adaption was essential to the survival of our species. Species that could not adapt and evolve to the changing world around them were unable to survive and reproduce, leading to the extinction of the species. The ability to adapt was the secret to our ancestor's survival and success!

In the same way, an ability to adapt and a willingness to embrace change is the secret to human success in the modern world! Those who are able to adapt and willing to embrace change are able to get ahead and enjoy success in the 21st century! George Bernard Shaw once said this: 'Progress is impossible without change, and those who can't change their minds cannot change anything'.

Whether we like it or not, we live in a world of change. At all times, things are constantly changing and transforming. We, therefore, have two options: we can resist change and refuse to embrace progression, or we can choose to embrace change as a positive opportunity for personal growth instead! For the sake of your continued success and flourishing, you have got to get comfortable with change!

In order to thrive in life, you need to be prepared to embrace new technologies, consider new ideas, and try out new ways of working. The world isn't going to grind to a halt just because you are stuck in your ways! Society is continually evolving and transforming, and if you refuse to embrace this change, it is you who will pay the price and get left behind.

That's why it is essential to stop clinging onto how things are now and confidently look forward to how they might be tomorrow. Change is nothing to fear! Change will not ruin your life or take away your happiness! On the contrary, change is a positive catalyst for personal development and growth!

Change presents us with amazing new opportunities to grow, flourish and thrive! As Winston Churchill once remarked, 'to improve is to change; to be perfect is to change often'.

Remember that life is all about progress, evolution, and development. Stop fearing change and see it as a positive opportunity to grow instead!

Instead of unsuccessfully fighting against evolution, choose to embrace progression! Instead of resisting change and transformation, choose to grow and thrive as a result of them instead!

Use change to your advantage by growing through what you go through and giving everything a go! Stay committed to your core values whilst confidently embracing change! See societal change as a positive catalyst for fulfilling your potential in life!

42 STOP LIVING SUPERFICIALLY

Since the beginning of Western philosophy, philosophers have been warning about the dangers of unbridled pleasures and superficial living. In his Ancient Greek writing, Plato has Socrates warn against unbridled passion and urge that a higher form of beauty be pursued.

In the 19th century, John Stuart Mill wrote that people must pursue 'higher pleasures' such as reading, classical music or philosophizing, and avoid the temptation of the 'lower pleasures', such as greed and lust. He wrote that 'it is better to be Socrates dissatisfied than a pig satisfied', suggesting that true happiness is the result of pursuing intelligent and civilised pleasures, rather than indulging in animalistic and overly-physical desires.

Whilst there is absolutely nothing wrong with enjoying a little bit of physical pleasure, there is nothing to be gained from becoming a slave to physical desire. A life driven by greed, lust and physical desire is a deeply unfulfilling and empty life indeed! As human beings, we need something more substantial and meaningful than the satisfaction of our basic physical desires. Man cannot live on bread, sex and physical pleasure alone! We need to nourish our hearts, souls and minds just as much as our bodies! We need to fulfil our intellectual and spiritual appetites just as much as our physical ones!

If you want to experience genuine happiness and a deep sense of fulfilment, you need to stop living superficially! That means striving to go beyond your physical desires and aspiring to create a deeply meaningful life instead! Instead of living as a slave to your physical passions and living a life driven by insatiable greed and untameable lust, strive to connect with a higher purpose and enjoy the 'higher pleasures' of life.

Realise that you can move beyond the superficial and achieve genuine spiritual, moral and human fulfilment. Live the deeply fulfilling and genuinely enriching existence that you deserve to live! And never reduce the quality of your life down to your enjoyment of primitive physical pleasures again! You are so much more than that!

43 YOU ARE PERFECTLY IMPERFECT

Roy Bennett once said this: "Embrace being perfectly imperfect. Learn from your mistakes and forgive yourself… you'll be happier". Nobody is perfect and – more importantly - nobody needs to be. Every single person is imperfectly imperfect! Every single human has unconditional value and worth! You don't need to be perfect in order to be loved, valuable or have worth. Remember that life is all about progress and not perfection!

Steven Naraboli said this: 'Stop trying to 'fix' yourself; you're NOT broken! You are perfectly imperfect and powerful beyond measure'. You are perfect, just as you are. You do not need to be fixed or cured. Instead, you need to be proud of who you authentically are! You are broken, you are vulnerable, you are flawed…and it's beautiful!

Our fragility and our failings make us the beautiful humans we should be proud to be! You are not loved for being perfect and flawless…you are loved precisely because you are not! You are broken and that's why you're beautiful!

As the late Stephen Hawking is quoted as once saying: 'One of the basic rules of the universe is that nothing is perfect. Perfect simply doesn't exist…without imperfection, neither you nor I would exist'. Embrace the fact you are perfectly imperfect. Don't be so afraid of your flaws and vulnerabilities. They are not weaknesses or anything to be ashamed of – they are what make you an amazing human being!

You are loved and valued because of your flaws and fallibilities, not despite them. You are broken, and it is beautiful! Dare to live your truth, let people get to know the real you, and celebrate the fact you are perfectly imperfect!

44 ASPIRE TO INSPIRE

Make it your mission in life to 'aspire to inspire'. Through your words and actions, you have the opportunity to make an extraordinarily positive difference in other people's lives. In everything that you do, you have the chance to empower, motivate and inspire countless people around you. Let your authenticity and achievement become a source of inspiration for other people!

In life, do whatever you can to help and support the people you meet as you go through life! Wherever you go, leave a positive legacy behind you! Whatever you do, strive to do it in a way that will inspire and empower anybody following in your footsteps.

Remember: we always have a choice over the contents of our lives. On the one hand, we can choose to live a life fixated on the acquisition of personal possessions, rewards and validation. There's nothing wrong with living this kind of self-centred life, as long as it genuinely makes you happy and you are not causing anybody else any harm.

But on the other hand, we can choose to live a life inspired by the mantra 'aspire to inspire'. We can strive to be a positive presence, make a positive difference, and leave a positive legacy everywhere we go. We can strive to empower and inspire every single person that we meet, and we can take our opportunity to be a role model for others seriously.

Brendan Burchard put it like this: 'As soon as you seek to inspire others, it inspires the best in you'. Remember, success in life is not just what we accomplish for ourselves, but about what we inspire others to do as well.

One important final point: you don't need to be perfect in order to inspire others. Quite the opposite! As Robert Tew puts it: 'Let people get inspired by how you deal with your imperfections'. When you dare to be vulnerable and you dare to talk about traditionally taboo topics, you become the greatest inspiration and beacon of light for others.

Indeed, when you share your authentic story and open up about your struggles, you give the people around you hope and reassurance that they're going to be okay.

So dare to be a leader who starts these difficult conversations and lights up the world! Dare to be someone who motivates, liberates and empowers people everywhere you go!

45 WHAT OTHER PEOPLE THINK OF YOU IS IRRELEVANT

People don't have to like you, and you don't have to care. Yes, it's really that simple! As human beings, we waste far too much time worrying about what other people think of us! We waste far too much energy trying to please and impress utterly irrelevant other people! It's time to stop outsourcing your validation to other people, and it's time to start living life on your own terms instead!

Of course, it's nice to be liked. But it's even better to be respected. And the easiest way to earn respect is to act like somebody who likes themselves, irrespective of what other people think or say. The truth of the matter is this: you can never please everybody. More to the point, you should never want to please everybody!

As long as you are happy with who you are, that should be all that matters! That's not to say that you shouldn't ever take other people's feedback and advice, which can often be very helpful and insightful. However, it does mean that you should never be dependent on external validation in order to feel good about yourself. And you certainly shouldn't become a spineless people-pleaser, who sleepwalks through life as a slave to other people's opinions.

In the words of Winston Churchill: 'You have enemies? Good. That means you've stood up for something, sometime in your life'. Instead of worrying about whether people you don't know like you, focus on living in accordance with your core values and standing up for the moral principles you believe in.

Living in accordance with your moral principles – rather than aimlessly people-pleasing – is the secret to a happy and fulfilling life!

It's hard, but you've just got to accept the fact that not everybody is going to like you. No matter how hard you try, you are never going to be every single person's cup of tea. But that's nothing to worry about! You don't need to be universally liked in order to be a good, worthwhile and valuable human being!

Remember: as long as you are not causing anybody any harm, you do not need to worry about what anybody thinks about you! Indeed, what other people think of you is actually none of your business! Instead, you should focus on doing good deeds, pursuing your own happiness, and becoming the best version of yourself.

Be too busy living in accordance with your core values to care about what irrelevant outsiders might think! They're entitled to think what they like about you, and you're entitled to pay their opinions no attention whatsoever.

Don't let other people dictate how you feel about yourself! Because whilst people don't have to like you, you don't have to care! Just because one person doesn't like you, that doesn't mean you are fundamentally unlikeable or should not like yourself! I cannot emphasise this to you enough: as long as you are not causing anybody any harm, you have absolutely nothing to apologise for!

Remember: there is not a single person on this planet who is universally liked. In the same way we all prefer different foods, we all prefer different kinds of people. Don't take it personally if you're not one person's flavour of the month!

And don't get all of your validation from other people's approval or being popular! Instead, get your validation from living in accordance with your own core values.

Integrity and authenticity are so much more important than popularity! At the end of the day, it all comes down to this: in order to live a happy life, you don't need to be liked by everybody else…you just need to like yourself.

46 ACCEPT YOUR EMOTIONS

It's amazing how many people feel uncomfortable around their own emotions. Are you one of the millions of people who fear facing their feelings? Do you have a tough time accepting and acknowledging your emotions? Do you worry that you won't be able to cope with certain emotions if you give them space to surface?

Here's what you need to know: your emotions are nothing to be scared of. Your feelings are nothing to be afraid of. You are more than capable of acknowledging, accepting and managing all of your emotions. Your emotions may be strong, but you are stronger! They are only capable of overwhelming you if you let them…and, by learning to acknowledge and accept them, you can ensure they are never able to overwhelm you! And so, it's time to start radically and unconditionally accepting every single one of your emotions. It's time to realise that every single one of your feelings is 100% valid!

Lori Deschene said this: 'You don't have to be positive all the time. It's perfectly okay to feel sad, angry, annoyed, frustrated, scared, or anxious. Having feelings does not make you a 'negative person'. It makes you human'.

Get serious about making space for all of your feelings and emotions. Allow them to exist and fully accept them for what they are. Instead of struggling and fighting against them, take a genuine interest in them! Keep an open mind and remember that allowing yourself to feel emotion does not mean you're going to lose control of your life.

Letting an emotion or feeling exist does not mean it is going to overwhelm you and ruin your life! Just because you made space for that emotion, this doesn't mean it's going to take over your entire existence!

Instead, making space for this emotion is going to enrich your existence, because it's going to allow you to cultivate self-awareness and gain insight into who you are.

That's because, by observing our emotions, we can learn more about what makes us tick as human beings. And, by accepting our emotions, we can take full responsibility for all of our thoughts, feelings and emotions. We become stronger, wiser, and more resilient than ever before!

Make space for your emotions! Make an effort to become a neutral observer of your feelings, rather than becoming overwhelmed by them. Let your emotions just come and go, rather than suppressing or becoming a slave to them!

Stop fighting your feelings and make an effort to unconditionally accept all of your emotions instead. Allow them to show up and show you something. When you stop struggling against them, you develop the capability to accept, understand and even harness them! Don't be afraid of your emotions – strive to live with emotional intelligence instead!

47 IT'S OKAY TO BE DIFFERENT

Standing out and daring to be different takes an extraordinary amount of courage. It goes against the natural human desire to blend in and take refuge in the larger group. As theologian Karen Keen writes, "Human beings appear to have an innate desire for sameness. Studies show we are attracted to people who look similar to us – we gravitate toward those who have the same opinions and interests. Our beliefs are not formulated by facts as much as by a desire to blend into a social group".

She continues: "Most of us will hide or minimise differences in order to avoid jeopardizing our insider status. Fear of losing our place of belonging is a primary motivation for our reaction to difference. When something unusual appears on the scene, we naturally want to protect our group's cohesion and equilibrium. This leads to targeting almost any difference for expulsion or forced conformity, even if it poses no real harm". Keen gives the example of the hostility traditionally directed towards the 10% of people who are left-handed in society.

Being different is nothing to be afraid of. Being authentic is actually the most amazing and empowering thing in the world. As John Stuart Mill once wrote, 'it is only the cultivation of individuality which can produce well developed human beings'. Being different is nothing to fear or apologise for. Instead, it is something to celebrate and embrace!

So dare to be different and allow your uniqueness to illuminate the world! Never compromise on your individuality in order to conform to someone else's preferences or expectations.

Be proud of who you are, not ashamed of how someone else sees you. Have the confidence to live a fearlessly authentic life!

48 CONFIDENCE LOOKS GOOD ON YOU

Confidence is the most attractive thing you can wear. In the words of Coco Chanel, 'beauty begins the moment you decide to be yourself'. Never mind the designer brands and labels…no amount of money can buy the attractiveness that carrying yourself with confidence delivers!

Carrying yourself with confidence is like a magnet for success. When you step outside with the mindset, body language and aura of somebody who is secure in their own skin, you instantly attract success and good fortune into your life! This good fortune will begin overflowing in every single area of your life, whether that is your love life, social life, career or personal finances.

When you start acting like you know what you're doing and know what values you stand for, people will instantly be drawn to you. Potential employers will be impressed by your interview performance, whilst potential lovers will want to ask you on that second date. Confidence really is the key to success in every single area of your life!

That's because confidence conveys competence and suggests self-security. And people are attracted to those individuals who are secure in their own skin and assertive about their identity!

Whenever you step outside, make it your mission to exude self-confidence. Present yourself as the secure and resilient human being that you are! Totally own your identity, and act like somebody who actually likes themselves!

Of course, it is important to remember there is a massive difference between genuine self-confidence and arrogance. Being 'secure' is very different from having an 'attitude' or 'ego'. Thinking you are better than everyone else, for example, will only result in you looking very insecure and immature. Human beings do not warm to rude or arrogant people…at all!

Remember this: confidence is not 'they will like me'. Instead, confidence is 'I'll be fine if they don't'. It means liking yourself unconditionally, without worrying for one second about what other people think. It means living with a sense of purpose and an awareness of your core values as an authentic individual.

At every opportunity, exude genuine self-confidence and self-security. At first, you might have to 'fake it until you make it'. But the more you 'wear' self-confidence, the easier it will become.

My top tip on self-confidence is this: try not to think about it too much. If you allow yourself to become consumed with worry, you'll never leave the front door. If you want to live with confidence, you've just got to get out there and own it! Dare to do more of the things that scare you and you'll find that you're becoming more and more self-confident by the second! When it comes to cultivating self-confidence, learning on the job is the secret to success! Never mind taking the theory test, this project is 100% practical!

Confidence looks good on you! So live your truth, live with self-confidence, and start attracting all of that goodness you deserve into your life!

49 PURSUE YOUR PASSIONS

If you want to find fulfilment in life, then you have got to get serious about pursuing your passions. You have got to start doing more of the things that bring you genuine happiness, fulfilment and flourishing in your life!

Ask yourself this: what am I truly passionate about? What topics, hobbies, activities or causes genuinely interest me? What things make me feel alive and bring a real sense of joy to my life?

When you have discovered what makes you tick, and when you have identified what things you are most passionate about, you need to get serious about pursuing these passions! Life is too short to be wasted doing things that drain you! It is essential that you invest time, effort, and energy into doing things that set your soul on fire!

Nothing is more important than pursuing your passions. They enrich your life, illuminate your existence, and ignite your soul. Make more time for the things that make you feel truly alive! Do more things that bring you genuine happiness, joy, and fulfilment!

Fill your days with the activities and pursuits that bring purpose to your life! This is the fastrack to living a genuinely fulfilling and enriching existence! If you want to live your very best life and fulfil your potential as a human being, you need to make pursuing your passions your priority!

50 MAINTAIN A ROUTINE

If you want to be more productive in your life, then you need to get serious about creating – and maintaining – a routine! Nothing is more important than creating a daily or weekly schedule…and then sticking to it!

Healthy habits are the fundamental foundations of a productive, successful and fulfilling existence. When you implement routine and introduce positive daily habits, you totally transform the quality of your life. As Aristotle once famously remarked, 'We are what we repeatedly do. Excellence, then, is not an act, but a habit'.

If you want to get more out of your day, then you need to make healthy habits and maintaining a positive routine your new number one priority! Creating a routine – for example, getting up and going to bed at the same time each day - allows you to get maximum productivity out of your day. When you sort out your schedule, you sort out your life!

Just think about it: how much time do you waste procrastinating or trying to decide what to do? How many hours go by without having absolutely anything to show for them? How many times do you find yourself rushing around and stressing out because, yet again, you've left everything to the very last minute?

The best way to live a motivated, fulfilling and successful life is by implementing healthy habits, introducing a daily routine…and then stick to them! This might mean getting up at the same time every day, striving to drink a certain amount of water, or making time to meditate before you go to bed each evening. Whatever you decide to do, make sure you are disciplined about it!

When you get serious about taking care of your schedule and routine, you totally revolutionise your life! You find that you get so much more done, and you find that you feel so much more in control of your life. So get serious about creating a schedule, sticking to routines…and start living your most positive and productive life imaginable. All that you need is a diary (either a physical diary or one of your phone) and a little bit of self-discipline!

51 CHOOSE QUALITY OVER QUANTITY

The 19th-century philosopher John Stuart Mill saw happiness as the most important aim of human existence. He was a famous proponent of Utilitarianism, a popular moral theory which states human beings should act to maximise the 'greatest happiness of the greatest number'. Mill believed that human beings should make the pursuit of pleasure a priority in their lives.

However, Mill was very clear that humans must take the quality of the pleasure into account, rather than simply focusing on the quantity. Indeed, Mill differentiated between two different types of pleasure – higher pleasures and lower pleasures. Higher pleasures, such as intellectual conversation or philosophizing, were intrinsically better than lower pleasures, such as sex or alcohol.

Mill famously declared that it is 'better to be a human being dissatisfied than a pig satisfied'. Mill believed that anyone with experience of the higher pleasures in life – which are chiefly intellectual - would automatically prefer them to the lower pleasures, which are primarily physical.

The higher pleasures typically have a higher purpose behind them, whereas the lower pleasures are often animalistic and based on primitive desires such as lust or greed. Thus, Mill encourages us all to recognise the importance of quality over quantity!

The more we pursue the 'higher pleasures' in life, the closer we come to fulfilling our potential and thriving as a human being. When it comes to your happiness and enjoyment of pleasure in life, always consider the quality just as much (if not more than!) the quantity!

An endless indulgence in solely 'lower pleasures' – those fuelled by animalistic and primitive desires – will never bring you the satisfaction or fulfilment you crave. On the other hand, the pursuit of the 'higher pleasures' of the intellect and soul will endlessly enrich your life!

Apply the quality over quantity rule to every area of your life: apply it to how you measure everything from friendships to how much time you spend revising for exams!

Remember that value and success is gained through quality, not quantity! Stop focusing on the mass-produced and make sure everything you do is meaningful!

52 PEACE COMES FROM WITHIN

'Peace comes from within. Do not seek it without'. These words, attributed to the Buddha, carry so much significance in our appearance and external validation obsessed world. In a society that appears to believe happiness and fulfilment can be commercialised, bought and sold, it is essential to remind ourselves that our souls are not for sale! Just as important as the clothes you are wearing, and the products you are buying is the contents of our character!

Here's what I strongly believe: no matter how much you consume, achieve or do, you will never find true happiness in life unless you have genuine inner peace within your own soul.

You cannot find inner peace or genuine happiness in the wider world if you do not have them within your own soul first. No amount of designer labels or social media followers can compensate for lack of inner peace within your heart!

Instead of always trying to show off or win external validation, it is essential that you prioritise achieving inner peace within your own soul. Does your soul feel nourished and fulfilled? Do you feel content, secure and peaceful within your own skin? Is there a sense of calm and confidence that radiates from within your heart?

Make time to cultivate inner peace within your soul. That might mean spending some time practising meditation or investing some time figuring out who you are and what you value the most in your life. It might mean removing yourself from situations or social media platforms that are causing you more harm than good and making an effort to do more of the things that soothe your soul.

Ultimately, inner peace means unconditionally accepting who you authentically are and consistently living life in accordance with your core values. It means knowing you have integrity, principles and unconditional worth as a human being. And it means knowing you are unequivocally enough, irrespective of what you do – or do not – have.

Unless you are anchored by inner peace, you will spend your entire life like a little sailing ship caught in a storm at sea. No matter what you gain or achieve in the world, you will never find true contentment or calm unless you have found genuine peace and self-acceptance within your own soul.

Aspire to enjoy your own company and strive to genuinely accept who you authentically are. Stop obsessing about external validation and worldly gain. Stop trying to buy your way to contentment.

Instead, just for a moment, consider how you can find peace within your own very soul. In a world obsessed with consumption and appearances, try to remember that peace ultimately comes from within. Inner peace is absolutely everything, so make sure you make it your absolute priority!

53 LIFE IS ABOUT BECOMING THE BEST VERSION OF YOURSELF

Make it your life's mission to become the very best version of yourself. Strive to fulfil your potential, make a positive difference, and make your life meaningful. Instead of constantly aspiring to have more in life, aspire to become more as a human being. Make it your purpose in life to keep growing as an individual. .

Make a commitment to making the most of your precious time here on this planet. Seize every opportunity to become the very best possible version of your authentic self. See this lifetime as your chance to fulfil your potential and flourish as a human being. Remember, you were not just born to survive – you were born to thrive!

Abraham Maslow's famous hierarchy of needs theory teaches us that 'self-actualisation' is the highest level of psychological development. According to Maslow, self-actualisation is the ability to become the best version of yourself.

He said this: 'This tendency might be phrased as the desire to become more and more what one is, to become everything that one is capable of becoming'. According to Maslow, so-called 'self actualisers' share the ability to achieve peak experiences, moments of pure joy, and transcendence. Self-actualisers tend to be highly creative, autonomous, objective, concerned about humanity and accepting.

Of course, self-actualisation looks like different things to different people. Every single one of us is a unique and autonomous individual with a personal conception of 'success' and 'happiness'. That's precisely why self-actualisation is all about becoming the best version of YOU – it is about fulfilling **your** unique and self-determined purpose in life!

That could be absolutely anything, such as becoming a parent, being a good friend, doing a job that you genuinely enjoy, or even travelling around the world! The specifics are entirely subjective to your personal preferences! The important thing is that you striving to become the very best version of yourself within the circumstances that you find yourself in!

Make it your mission to be the best version of you in every situation that you find yourself in. Make it your daily goal to become a better person than you were yesterday. Make personal growth your absolute priority in life!

Wherever you're up to in life, strive to do your best and be the best version of yourself. Wherever you go and whatever you do, make it your mission to keep growing as an authentic and autonomous human being! Remember – the only person you should ever compete with in life is who you were yesterday!

54 STOP REACTING AND START RESPONDING

Life is 10% what happens to you and 90% how you choose to respond. Whatever happens in your life, you always have a choice over how you respond!

Whilst it's very easy to impulsively react to everything that happens to us, this is a very unintelligent way of living. It leaves us at the mercy of our circumstances and as a slave to our emotional impulses. As a result, we end up losing all control over our lives and constantly careering from one crisis to another. We give rude and unkind people power over our mood and lose sight of what's truly important in our lives! As a result, we lose all autonomy over our own existence. Impulsively reacting to situations is, in short, nothing but a recipe for disaster!

But guess what? You're life doesn't have to be this way! You don't need to step your life at the mercy of your circumstances and as a slave to your emotions! Instead of impulsively reacting to whatever happens in your life, you can learn to start intelligently responding instead! When you learn the art of pausing, reflecting, and really thinking about how you will respond to situations, you absolutely transform your life! You finally put yourself firmly back in the driving-seat of your life! You are able to shape the future of your own existence, rather than continuing to live as a victim of your circumstances and at the mercy of your unpredictable emotions!

Viktor Frankl explains it like this: 'Between stimulus and response there is a space. In that space is our power to choose our response. In our response lies our freedom and our growth'.

Never forget the power that you possess to consciously choose your response. It is in exercising power to choose that you find freedom, autonomy and growth.

55 UNDERSTAND WHO YOU ARE

Everywhere we look in the world there are experts on just about everything. There are experts on everything from meteorology, fashion and ancient history, to art, gardening and football! But whilst there is an endless supply of experts on everything from the solar system to group sports, very few people are experts on themselves!

According to Aristotle, one of the founding fathers of Western Philosophy, 'knowing yourself is the beginning of all wisdom'. Indeed, self-awareness and self-knowledge are the fundamental foundations for a deeply fulfilling life.

Whilst many of us might spend our lives taking selfies, very few of us have any real self-awareness into who we are or what makes us tick. We don't make an effort – or perhaps we don't have the confidence – to look beyond the surface level of our outer appearances and explore what is driving us as human beings.

As a result, so many of us spend our lives stuck in a cycle of making the same mistakes, believing the same self-limiting beliefs, and getting ourselves into the same toxic situations…again and again!

You don't have to keep living your life in a state of introspective ignorance! You don't have to keep your head buried in the sand! There is another way!

Instead of living in ignorance, you can get serious about cultivating self-awareness. There's an old saying that the greatest challenge in life is discovering who you are, and the second greatest is being happy with what you find.

Socrates, one of the wisest men to have ever lived, had two simple words of wisdom for his followers: know thyself. There you have the secret to a successful life in a nutshell! If you want to live an enlightened and enjoyable existence, make it your mission to know who you are!

Know who you are, what you stand for, and what you want from life. Get serious about introspection and self-awareness, and I guarantee that you will totally revolutionise your life.

By gaining introspective insight into who we are, we illuminate and enrich our lives. With self-awareness, we become unstoppable forces for good on our journey to living our very best lives!

56 BE CLEAR ABOUT YOUR BOUNDARIES

Always be clear about your boundaries. The secret to a successful life is setting clear and consistent boundaries. When you implement clear boundaries, you boost your self-esteem, conserve your emotional energy, and gain more independence as a human being. Through boundaries, we assert our worth and become autonomous agents in our own lives.

Brene Brown said this: 'Daring to set boundaries is about having the courage to love ourselves, even when we risk disappointing others'. Setting boundaries is a supreme – and essential – act of self love. It is all about having the courage to put yourself first and recognising what you deserve in life. It means recognising your needs as an individual and daring to live your life on your own terms.

Remember: in life, you only get what put up with. Boundaries allow you to outline what you will – and will not – put up with from other people. Without these boundaries, people are free to walk all over you! We need boundaries in order to clarify what kind of treatment we expect and will tolerate in our relationships. We also need boundaries to ensure that we are aligning our time choices with our core values as human beings!

Boundaries are all about increasing our assertiveness, safeguarding our spaces, conserving our emotional energy and – most importantly – knowing our worth. With boundaries, you become capable of saying 'no' and you become confident at walking away from situations – and people – that are not meeting your expectations or respecting your value as an individual. Never feel bad about asserting your boundaries and being strict about sticking to them! At all times just remember this: the only people upset about you having boundaries are the people who benefit from you having none.

Be clear about your boundaries. Don't compromise on your red lines. Set your standards high, protect your time, and become capable of saying 'no'! Remember that you only ever get what you put up with! Set out your core boundaries...and religiously stick to them! Know your worth and assert yourself as a self-respecting, autonomous adult! Live an autonomous and assertive life!

57 STEP OUTSIDE OF YOUR COMFORT ZONE

Your comfort zone is – as the name suggests – a very comfortable place. It's somewhere we feel very safe, settled and secure. It's a place where we feel coated in bubble wrap and protected from the world. This is all well and good, and I don't blame anyone who is quite content living within the confines of their comfort zone! But here's the thing you need to know: a comfort zone is a beautiful place, but nothing ever grows there.

That's because, although the comfort zone may be a very comforting place, life only begins when you dare to step outside of your comfort zone. Indeed, everything you have ever wanted is one step outside of your comfort zone.

The question I have to ask you is this: will you dare to put yourself out there and boldly step outside of your comfort zone? Will you dare to leave behind your safety bubble and see what happens when you risk putting yourself out there in the world beyond your comfort zone?

In the words of Thomas Jefferson: 'If you want something you've never had, you must be willing to do something you've never done'. You cannot expand and enrich your life if you keep on living within the confines of your comfort zone. If you want to experience greater success and flourishing than ever before, you need to take more risks and dare to put yourself out there. If you're not prepared to be challenged, then you're never going to be able

to grow! Without risks, there is no growth. And without growth, there is no success or flourishing!

Remember, whatever happens in your life – you can handle it. Every 'risk' you take is actually a win-win situation! So why are you still holding yourself back? Why are you still imposing limitations and restrictions on your existence?

Dare to take risks, step outside your comfort zone, and enlarge your life! Remember, growth begins at the end of your comfort zone! Cultivate confidence, leave your comfort zone behind…and enjoy more success than you ever thought imaginable!

Are you feeling scared? Good! That's a sign you are not only growing but that you are on the verge of achieving extraordinary levels of success as well! So feel that fear…and do it anyway! You were not born to hide away in your comfort zone…you were born to thrive outside of it!

Dare to step outside and your comfort zone and start living your very best life today! Remember that whatever happens, you can handle it. Enlarge your life and enrich your existence by daring to move beyond the boundaries of your comfort zone. Dare to that risk and I guarantee that you will reap the rewards!

58 STOP FEARING FAILURE

To what extent do you let your fears rule over your life? How often do you limit and restrict yourself because you're worried about what could go wrong?

As human beings, we are naturally cautious about things that could go wrong. We are hardwired to identify potential threats and risks in the environment around us, allowing us to protect ourselves and defend our tribes. It's very good to have an awareness of these potential risks and dangers – back in our ancestor's tribal days, being alert to potential threats was literally a matter of life or death!

However, whilst it's important to be aware of potential threats and dangers, it is equally as important not to become paralysed by them! To put it another way, it is important to acknowledge fear without being limited by it. In the words of Susan Jeffers, you've got to 'feel the fear…and do it anyway!'

Just because failure is a possibility, this doesn't mean it is inevitable. Just because things could go wrong, this doesn't mean they will. Why are you spending your life anticipating failure and dwelling on what could go wrong, when you could just as easily be focusing on what could actually go right and work out well? And, even if things do wrong and you end up failing at something, remember that you are more than capable of surviving absolutely any setbacks that you face in your life!

Remember that, whatever happens in your life, you can handle it! Every setback is a stepping stone towards success! When you start to think like this, you start to realise that taking risks is actually a win-win scenario. And, as a result, a fear of failure will no longer be able to paralyse you!

Even if everything does go wrong, you're going to be okay! So dare to take those risks, step outside of your comfort zone, and confront your fear of failure!

When you live with a growth mindset and see every setback as a stepping stone towards success, you'll find that it is actually impossible to fail at absolutely anything!

59 GRATITUDE LEADS TO GREATNESS

Albert Einstein once said this: 'There are only two ways to live your life. One is as though nothing is a miracle. The other is as though everything is a miracle'. Gratitude with gratitude is all about seeing everything in life as a gift! It means appreciating every person, possession, opportunity, and experience in your existence! And it means cherishing each day as a divinely-gifted chance to express thanks for your life and your loved ones!

GK Chesterton put it best when he wrote that 'When it comes to life, the critical thing is whether you take things for granted or take them with gratitude'. In our 21st-century consumption culture, it's so easy to take everything in our lives for granted.

As a result, we are constantly feeling unfulfilled and as if what we have is never enough. If only we started living with an attitude of gratitude! How quickly we would realise that our lives are already filled with an abundance of things to be thankful for! As Meister Eckhart taught, 'if the only prayer you said was thank you, that would be enough'.

Some people mistakenly believe that gratitude can be delayed. They think that they can only start having 'gratitude' for their life once they're multi-millionaires living in a 12-bedroom mansion.

This approach to gratitude is completely wrong! Your practice of gratitude and appreciation must begin right here and right now! If you cannot appreciate what you have right now, you will never be satisfied with what you might gain in the future. As a result, you will never find happiness or contentment in your life. In the words of John Candy, 'if you're not happy without it, you'll never be happy with it'.

As Melanie Beattie says, 'Gratitude turns what we have into enough'. In a culture obsessed with constant consumption and wealth comparison, practising gratitude for life's simple pleasures is a very radical act! It is only when we realise that the 'rat race' is not fulfilling us that we can free ourself from the 'never enough' mentality and start appreciating the gifts of our lives instead! Gratitude is all about seeing the world as a gift, rather than taking it for granted. When we start seeing the world as this gift, the entire quality of our lives is transformed. Indeed, an attitude of appreciation will enrich and illuminate your life. It will totally transform the quality of your entire existence!

I'm a great believer that gratitude is the great multiplier. The more than you express gratitude, the more that you will attract more things to be grateful for into your life! That's in stark contrast to the 'never enough' mentality, where addiction to consumption and comparison leaves us feeling more unfulfilled and unhappy than ever before.

Instead of constantly trying to gain more externally, try to have more gratitude internally. In an almost paradoxical way, being satisfied with less means that you will gain more than you could have ever possibly imagined! As Eckhart Tolle once said: 'Acknowledging the good that you already have in your life is the foundation for all abundance'.

As Cicero taught over 2,000 years ago, 'gratitude is not only the greatest of virtues but the parent of all others'. Goodness in your life all begins with gratitude! And so, if you only do one thing today, ensure that it's making a commitment to living with gratitude! Remember, gratitude is a choice! Seize this opportunity to live a life overflowing with gratitude, and you will instantly start reaping the rewards!

Get serious about living with a grateful heart and approaching each day with a spirit of appreciation! Be thankful for everything – both small and big, good and bad – and thank the universe for every opportunity, obstacle, simple pleasure, and life lesson that it sends you!

The last word goes to Rhonda Byrne, who said this: "Gratitude will shift you to a higher frequency, and you will attract much better things".

60 MARGINAL GAINS MAKE ALL THE DIFFERENCE

Transformation in life does not happen overnight. What appears to be an overnight success has really been many years in the making! Whilst there may be many TV shows and advertising campaigns talking about 'overnight transformations', the reality is that transformation takes time if you want to change your life for good – and not for a week or so! – then you need to focus on marginal gains, rather than major overnight revolutions.

The philosophy of 'marginal gains' is all about the small incremental improvements that add to a significant improvement when they are all added together. The idea is that, by making lots of little changes, we can make a massive change in our lives!

It's like the old saying 'look after the pennies, and the pounds will look after themselves!' When you focus on making lots of marginal gains, you'll start to see a major shift – that lasts forever! – in your life.

Jonathan Mills put it like this: 'Successful people demonstrate their resilience through their dedication to making progress every day, even if that progress is marginal'.

Remember, success is not achieved through grand gestures but through small steps instead. It is those incremental increases that create greatness! It is the daily practice, the tiny tweaks, and that commitment to perseverance that make all the difference!

Marginal gains mean focusing on making 1% improvements. These incremental increases may sound tiny on their own, but they soon add up and make a major difference!

Take a moment to think about the tiny changes and small improvements you might be able to make in your life today. It might be getting up 10 minutes earlier every morning to meditate, for example, or it might be having ½ a teaspoon less sugar in your cup of tea every morning. Remember, these small steps will end up making a massive difference! Tiny changes add up to bring about major transformations!

If you want to change your life, you need to stop buying into the 'overnight transformation' myth. If you want to bring about long-term change and transformation, get serious about making marginal gains.

Focus on those 1% improvements and guarantee yourself a lifetime of flourishing!

61 IN LIFE, YOU ONLY GET WHAT YOU PUT UP WITH

In life, you only ever get what you put up with. You are entirely responsible for how other people treat you. If you want respect, you've got to command it! If you want If you act like a doormat, then don't be surprised when other people start walking all over you! At all times, know your worth. At all times, hold your head up high and command the respect that you deserve.

Confucius said this: 'respect yourself and others will respect you'. I cannot emphasise this to you enough: you only get what you put up with in life! Whilst you can't force others to respect you – remember, you have no control over anything in life other than your own mindset and conduct – you can refuse to be disrespected!

If somebody mistreats you, don't roll over and let them do it to you again! You need to have the self-respect to know what kind of conduct you will – and will not – put up with! If you lie down on the floor and act like a doormat, don't be surprised when people walk all over you! In the same way, if you conduct yourself as a self-respecting adult, you will attract respect from people around you. It's a perfect equation!

The most important choice you can make for your life is this: choose to be a character who has self-respect. Keep your standards and expectations high. Don't let anybody make you feel worthless, stupid or insignificant. Live your life with self-respect, and remember that you only ever get what you put up with.

If somebody is putting you down or taking you for a fool, don't you dare put up with it! Instead, rise above their behaviour and remove them from your life.

Conduct yourself with dignity, self-respect and integrity. Refuse to tolerate anybody treating you badly. Give them an inch, and they will take a mile! You need to be firm and clear about commanding the respect that you deserve!

Wherever you go and whatever you do, hold your head up high and know your worth. Conduct yourself with kindness and dignity, treat other people how you would want to be treated. Prioritise integrity over popularity. Be true to your core values and moral principles. Remember that whilst it's nice to be liked or to feel loved, nothing is more important than being respected. If you don't have respect, you don't have anything.

And so, if somebody does not respect you as a human being, then do not let them into the inner circle of your life. Be polite, be friendly, and have a laugh with them. Approach them with a spirit of good-will and treat them how you would like to be treated. But do not be a fool and let them into your inner circle! Because if somebody cannot do something as simple as respect you, then they will not think twice before using, mistreating, and walking all over you. You cannot afford to invest precious effort or emotion in someone who clearly has no respecrt for you as a human being. Doing so would be like inviting a known thief into your home and then being shocked when they steal everything in your house!

Know very clearly what you will – and will not – tolerate or put up with. Be a character who has moral integrity and a strong understanding of accountability. Be assertive, be consistent, and be aware of what is going on around you. Remember that, in life, you only get what you put up with – and do not put up with anybody putting you down!

Always remember this: whilst you can't force others to respect you, but you can refuse to be disrespected. Nobody can make you feel inferior without your consent!

You don't have to tolerate anything you don't want or deserve in your life. You don't have to put up with anyone putting you down! If someone isn't treating you with respect, it is essential that you leave that situation or relationship with your head held high.

As Eleanor Roosevelt said, 'If someone betrays you once, it's your fault; if they betray you twice, it's your fault!'. Don't complain about something and then keep letting it happen! Have the self-confidence to say that enough is enough. Know what you deserve…nothing but absolute respect!

62 HAVE THE COURAGE TO BE DISLIKED

Don't spend your life as a prisoner to other people's opinions. Don't spend your life worrying about how you look or what other people are thinking about you. Remember, what other people think of you is none of your business! You cannot limit your life or hold yourself back because you are worried about what irrelevant strangers might think about you!

In order to live your very best life, you need to develop the courage to be disliked. Of course, it is always preferable to be liked…but it is not essential! You do not need to be universally liked in order to be a happy, fulfilled or successful human being! Just because somebody doesn't like you, that doesn't mean you have done anything wrong! Just because you are not one person's cup of tea, that doesn't mean you need to change who you are!

It's very simple: as long as you are not causing anybody any harm, then you do not need to change or apologise. So stop craving external validation and stop buying into the myth that it is either possible or indeed necessary to be universally liked! Remember this: there are plenty of good, happy and successful people on this planet…but there is not a single person on this world who is universally liked!

Remember, nothing is more important than being authentic and living your truth. If living your truth – as opposed to compromising on your core values and living a life of miserable conformity – means that a couple of people don't particularly like you,

In order to have the courage to be disliked, you need to like yourself. This all comes down to cultivating internal validation. This begins with developing self-awareness and self-acceptance. Do you like the person you are? Do you unconditionally accept yourself? Are you true to yourself? Are you proud of how you live your life? Instead of worrying about whether other people will like you, ask yourself this: do I genuinely like myself?

As long as you genuinely like yourself, and you are not causing other people harm, then you are guaranteed to live a genuinely happy and fulfilling life! The two actually go hand-in-hand: somebody who genuinely likes, accepts, and respects themselves will like, accept and respect other people. Happy people do not intentionally cause other people harm! And happy people do not take other people's rejection or rudeness to heart. That's because they are certain of their own worth and likeability, and so they do not need to see someone else's dislike of them as an end-of-the-world situation.

Instead, genuinely happy and self-confident individuals have the courage to be disliked! They are secure in the knowledge that whilst it's preferable to be liked, it is not essential. They do not depend on other people's acceptance in order to accept themselves. They realise that your worth as a human being does not depend on whether everybody you meet likes you! Just because you are not everybody's cup of tea, it is not the end of the world!

Live a fearlessly authentic life as the best version of yourself. Be kind, spread love, and do what you can to contribute to the common good of society. As long as you are doing your best and not causing anybody else any harm, then don't worry for a second what other people might think of you. This is your life! Remember, you do not need to be universally liked in order to like yourself.

Instead of desperately craving everybody's approval, fearlessly live life on your own terms and in accordance with your own values!

Instead of craving approval, surround yourself with authentic people who accept who you are and share in your core values!

Create a fulfilling life of conviction, not a superficial life of conformity! And, most importantly, don't take other people's dislike or disapproval to heart...it's not your fault they've got bad taste, is it now?!

63 NEVER CRITICISE, CONDEMN OR COMPLAIN

The first rule that Dale Carneige taught in his internationally bestselling book 'How to win friends and influence people' was this: never criticise condemn or complain. I strongly believe that, with this strict rule in mind, you cannot go far wrong in your social interactions.

When it comes to your social interactions, positivity is very important. You want to be known as somebody who lights up a room, not drains it of energy! Human beings are naturally attracted to anybody who radiates positivity and good energy – we love anybody who can make us laugh, make us smile, and make us feel good about ourselves. Become somebody who promotes good energy and people will be drawn to you like moths to a flame or bees swarming around honey!

On the other hand, people do not easily warm to anybody who is constantly being negative and putting other people down. Pessimism is a very repellent force – after all, who wants to be around anybody who is constantly complaining and criticising other people? Why would you spend time with somebody who is bitter and negative when you could spend time with someone in possession of a more optimistic outlook on life?

If you want to become a magnetic personality, make it your mission to be a positive presence. Keep an open mind, accept people, and live with optimism.

Seek to understand people and their actions, rather than just judge and condemn them. Seek to solve the difficult situations and problems you encountered, rather than just complaining about them. Strive to be constructive, rather than critical.

Try to confront life's challenges and bear life's burdens with a good sense of humour and optimistic attitude, rather than becoming known as a merchant of doom.

64 IT'S OKAY TO NOT BE OKAY

It's okay not to be okay. Feeling down or struggling with your mental health is nothing to be ashamed about. As the pop star, Jessie J is quoted to have said: 'it's healthy to admit you're not ok. It's 'ok not to be ok'. It's brave. But don't let it win. Be sad. Have your moment, your day or week. Then do something about it and be happy. For yourself".

And to quote Lori Deschene: 'You don't have to be positive all the time. It's perfectly okay to feel sad, angry, annoyed, frustrated, scared, or anxious. Having feelings does not make you a 'negative person'. It makes you human'.

Don't fight your feelings! Don't be embarrassed about your emotions! Every single feeling that your experience is valid. You are allowed to be emotional! You are allowed to feel upset! So be kind and compassionate to yourself! Seek to understand and make sense of your emotions, rather than trying to suppress them! Don't try to drown them out or lock them away! Be brave enough to make space for your emotions and feeling - acknowledge them and then work out ways to intelligently respond to them.

Here's how I see it: If everything isn't okay, that means it's not the end. Give yourself a moment to breathe and feel whatever it is that you're feeling. Everything is going to work out, but just not necessarily right now. And that's okay. It's normal to experience every single human emotion.

Suppression and denial will only result in even greater suffering down the line. So instead of fighting them, strive to intelligently observe and experience your emotions instead. Increase your tolerance of unpleasant emotions and realise that uncomfortable emotions are nothing to fear.

Know that asking for help is a sign of strength, not weakness. You don't have to go through this alone! Stop being ashamed or embarrassed about how you feel! You're only human after all! You're going to be okay, but it's okay if you're not on top form right now. Be kind to yourself and let other people help you during this tough time. You're going to get through this, but it's okay not to feel amazing right now. Take your time and talk about it. You're going to be okay.

65 A PROBLEM SHARED IS A PROBLEM SOLVED

A problem shared is a problem solved. Never suffer from anything in silence! You do not have to go through anything in life on your own! There are so many people in this world – even people you have never met – who want to support you. They want to provide you with a shoulder to cry on, a friendly face to turn to, and give you a non-judgemental space within which you can speak freely about whatever it is that's on your mind.

These people genuinely want to help you without expecting absolutely anything in return. They are not going to judge you or ridicule you – they just want to be there for you. My question to you is this: are you going to let them be there for you?

Asking for help is a sign of strength, not weakness. Talking about what how you're feeling or what you're going through is one of the most courageous things you can ever do. Nobody expects you to have a perfect life. Nobody expects you to cope with everything on your own.

Let your loved ones in, and let them help you to lighten the load. Remember, asking for help or admitting you're struggling is absolutely nothing to be ashamed of. It is instead one of the most courageous – not to mention lifechanging – things that you can ever do!

Whatever you're going through, you do not have to go through it alone. Share how you're feeling with someone you trust and let them be there for you during this tough time. Let them help you to lighten the load. Let them look out for you and give you a non-judgmental listening ear. Remember, they are not going to judge you or think less of you. Instead, they are going to unconditionally love you and be there for you! When we talk about how we're feeling or open up about what we're going through, we instantly lighten that load and feel a million times better in ourselves.

Always remember that you are not alone. Whatever you're going through, there are people who are here for you. Never be afraid to ask for help and never be ashamed about admitting you're going through a tough time right now. Whatever you do, don't suffer in silence. A problem shared is a problem solved.

If you need someone to talk to, the Samaritans are here to support you. Samaritans will not judge or tell you what to do. Whatever you're going through, you can call or email at any time for free. Call the Samaritans for free – at any time - on 116123 or email jo@samaritans.org (response time 24 hours).

66 YOU'RE DOING JUST FINE

Whatever you're doing, just remember that you're doing just fine. You're doing the best you can with what you have. You're making the most out of your current circumstances and conditions, and this is all that you can ever be expected to do.

In life, there is no need for everything to be perfect, and there is no pressure on you to perform. Stop worrying about whether you are doing enough or what other people might think of your performance. Stop comparing yourself to other people, and in particular what they choose to share on their social media.

Here's how I see it: each of us is on our own unique and personal journey through life. You never know what somebody has been through or what might be going on behind closed doors. And so, you can't compare someone else's social media highlights reel with your raw and real everyday life! This is your life and should be lived on your own terms in accordance with your own values.

Remember that life is not a race or competition! You have nothing to prove! Your worth does not need to be earned or won through achievements and appearances. Whatever you're doing is more than good enough. As I say, you're doing the best you can with what you have – and that is more than enough! You should not fall into the trap of constantly comparing your life or get into the habit of being excessively self-critical. Remember that you're only human! Remember that this is the real world, not a perfect utopia!

You are not living your life for the sake of impressing or pleasing other people. Life is not meant to be some kind of never-ending rat race. Instead, life is meant to be a beautiful and enjoyable journey.

Indeed, life is all about making memories, spreading love, and making a contribution to the common good. None of this requires perfectionism, and none of this justifies feelings of inadequacy or failure. Every moment of every day is a brand new opportunity to be yourself, connect with your core values, and appreciate the gift of your existence.

Remember, the simple fact that you are alive means that you are enough. So just keep breathing and keep bringing yourself back to the present moment. Take it day-by-day and just do what you can.

You are doing the best you can with what you have. And that is all that can ever be expected from you. So be kind to yourself and cut yourself some slack. Don't let airbrushed images on social media or unrealistic expectations from society deceive you!

You're doing just fine, so just keep on going and keep on being kind to yourself! Life, after all, is about progress, not perfection.

67 IF YOU WANT IT, WORK FOR IT

Don't pray for an easy life – work hard to create a meaningful one. Life is not meant to be a walk in the park, where everything is handed to you on a plate. Instead, life is meant to be a meaningful and purposeful journey of personal development!

If you're not happy about something, don't just complain about it – do something about it! Living a meaningful life is not about sitting around feeling sorry for yourself – it's all about working hard, growing through what you go through, and making a success out of whatever situation you find yourself in!

If you're not happy with your situation, don't just sit there and complain about it! Instead, roll up your sleeves and do what you can to improve it! Remember - if you want something in life, then you've got to work for it! You can't just complain about your circumstances and yet do absolutely nothing yourself to improve them! You can't expect to wake up one morning and find that all of your dreams have magically turned into your reality! If you want to transform your life, then you've got to put in the hard work yourself!

Remember that the process of working hard is just as important as the rewards we reap as a result of it. Indeed, we find our greatest amount of self-growth and flourishing in experiencing the process, not just enjoying the final product! Instead of complaining about your circumstances or dreaming of overnight success, make a commitment to waking up, working hard and putting your heart into achieving all of the things you dream of! Realise that life is all about making the best of what you've got,

If you want it, work for it. Roll out of bed, roll up those sleeves, and go get that bread! Work hard at turning your dreams into your reality! Enjoy the process of working hard, and then enjoy reaping the rewards later down the line!

Nothing in life is handed to us on a plate. The universe doesn't owe us anything! So stop feeling sorry about your situation and instead do something to improve it! Stop complaining and start creating! Make working hard to make the best of your circumstances your new number one priority!

68 ENJOY THE JOURNEY

Don't let a focus on your next destination distract you from enjoying the journey to getting there. Remember that the process is just as important as – if not more important than – the final product.

Enjoy the journey as much as the destination. Always remember that our lessons, enjoyment and personal growth always come from the journey, not the final destination!

We are at our happiest when we are creating, constructing, learning and working on things that we are passionate about! The process is so much more enriching, rewarding, and important than the destination we eventually arrive at! Indeed, you can only truly appreciate the product if you have appreciated and fully engaged with the journey to getting there!

Wherever you're going, always strive to enjoy the journey to getting there. Don't waste your life wishing you could arrive at some future destination. Don't delay your happiness or enjoyment of life until you arrive at some hypothetical finish line. Get serious about enjoying your life right here and right now!

 Get serious about enjoying the journey and embracing every twist, turn and diversion that you encounter on the way to your destination! The journey is what makes life meaningful and enjoyable, so don't wish it away!

So, enjoy every single step of your journey and completely throw yourself into thoroughly enjoying the process. Take things one day at a time. Seize every opportunity for self-growth and personal development! Whatever you're doing and wherever you're going in life, always remember to enjoy the journey!

69 RADICALLY ACCEPT THE UNIVERSE AS IT IS NOW

Stop struggling against reality! Stop complaining about how unfair life is! Stop wishing that were living in a fairytale and start making the most of what you've got in the real world! How often do you catch yourself complaining about life? How frequently do you find yourself drowning in self-pity about the fact life isn't fair? As human beings living in an unfair world, I believe that we have two very clear choices in life: we can choose to spend our lives complaining about the fact that life isn't fair, or we can choose to roll up our sleeves and get on with making the best out of our situations!

It's a fact of life that the world isn't fair, whatever 'fair' even means in the first place! In case you hadn't realised, we do not live in a perfect fairytale world, where the good guys all live happily ever after!

Instead, we live in a world where suffering is just a fact of everyday life. In the real world, thousands of innocent lives are lost to natural disasters, accidents and illnesses every single day. Rude, immoral and selfish people manage to cling onto wealth and power. There is never any guarantee that hard work or good deeds are going to be rewarded, at least not in this lifetime. We see unfairness all the time: colleagues who deserve promotions don't get them, students who deserve good grades miss out. Innocent children get bullied, innocent criminals get locked up. Relationships don't work out, we are lied to and deceived. The list of unjust and unfair examples could go on and on!

Here's the thing: whilst a wish for justice in this world is admirable, nobody actually promised you that life was going to be fair! Nobody guaranteed you that life was going to be a fairytale! Indeed, a quick observation of the natural world reveals that the universe is a rather cruel and merciless place to be. As JS

Mill once observed, 'nature commits all the crimes for which men would be hanged'. In the words of Thomas Hobbes, nature is in a state of 'war of all against all'. It's a cruel world out there! Instead of complaining that life isn't perfect, we need to be pragmatic about what we're really dealing with! We need to stop shielding ourselves from all the suffering in this world and learn to courageously face up to the reality of human existence.

Life is, I have to be clear about it, filled with suffering! We need to acknowledge and accept this, rather than continuing to deny it! There's no point continuing to deny or complain about the fact that life is tough. Instead, we need to be frank with ourselves and fully come to terms with the fact that the universe just isn't fair. Death, destruction and suffering are just facts of life! We need to radically accept – and make peace with – their existence! Once we've accepted this fact, we can learn to work with what we've got and make the most of the precious time, resources and opportunities that are available to us!

Indeed, once we stop struggling against suffering and courageously accept the world for what it is instead, we able to totally transform our lives! We learn to start working with what we've got and making the best of the circumstances we find ourselves in, rather than constantly struggling against them.

Try approaching life as a pragmatist, not as a perfectionist. Realise that life is filled with suffering and that there is nothing you can do about it…other than stop struggling against it! Stop complaining about the unfairness of the universe and start working with what you've got. Be a pragmatist who stoically bears life's burdens, rolls up their sleeves and makes the best out of every situation they find themselves in.

Accept the fact that life isn't fair. Stop wasting your precious time and energy struggling against reality. Instead, radically and wholeheartedly accept the reality of the world we live in. Meet the world where it is right now. Accept the world as it is and then take action to make the most of what you've got. Instead of complaining that 'it's not fair', be frank about the fact nobody promised you it would be. Do what you can to make the best out of your circumstances and make a positive difference in the world around you! Contribute to the common good and spread as much love, kindness and compassion as possible!

Make the most of the resources available to you! Stop wishing you were living in a fairy-tale and get serious about working with what you've got! Stop wishing your life away and start appreciating, enjoying and making the most of where you are right now! The universe isn't fair, but this doesn't have to faze you. Try to accept this fact and then make the best of what you've got in life.

70 THERE'S NOTHING WRONG WITH GETTING SOMETHING WRONG

In life, there are no mistakes or failures…there are only lessons learned! Our biggest mistakes of the past are our best teachers for the future! Our most challenging setbacks are the best stepping stones towards future success! Indeed, you need to fail and get things wrong in order to achieve future success and prosperity in your life!

Our cultural obsession with perfectionism and appearances means that we are terrified of getting things wrong. We want to protect ourselves from uncomfortable feelings such as embarrassment, fear, and shame. And so, we wrap ourselves in bubble wrap and go through life, hiding behind a mask. We don't take risks, we deploy countless defence mechanisms, and we obsess about our public appearance. We hide away in our comfort zone and become slaves to public opinion. The more that we do this, the unhappier we become. We lose sight of who we are and become prisoners to our fears. Life doesn't have to be this way! You don't have to spend your existence worrying about what people think or feeling terrified about getting things wrong!

Here's what you need to know: there's nothing wrong with getting something wrong! Making a mistake is not the end of the world! Getting rejected is not worse than death! Whatever happens in life, you can handle it. We need to make mistakes and get things wrong in order to grow! Failure is absolutely essential for our flourishing as human beings! So stop worrying about that mistake you made. And stop living life as a slave to your worries and fears. Dare to make those mistakes! Dare to risk getting rejected! Know that there's nothing wrong with getting something wrong! Whatever happens, you can handle it. So quit your imprisonment to perfection and roll up your sleeves…it's time to live your best possible life in this world!

71 LET IT COME, LET IT BE, LET IT GO

Everything in life is impermeant. Nothing in life – either good or bad – will ever stay the same. As the circle of life keeps turning, everything keeps changing. In order to find true happiness and contentment in life, we need to embrace the impermanence of existence, rather than fighting against it.

Whatever you are experiencing in life, remember this short mantra: 'Let it come, let it be, let it go'. Try not to resist reality or fight against the constantly evolving universe. Don't take anything too seriously and don't forget to keep everything into perspective. As the old saying goes, today's headline news is tomorrow's fish and chip paper! This situation will pass, and the world will keep on turning! So, do the best that you can with these circumstances, and then look forward to a new start tomorrow.

Nothing in this universe lasts forever. The tough time that you're going through right now will pass. Resolve to carry this temporary burden with as much calm, kindness, dignity and compassion as possible. Keep reminding yourself that nothing is more important – in this moment, or any other - than remembering to breathe!

In the words of Pema Chodron, 'Impermanence is a principle of harmony. When we don't struggle against it, we are in harmony with reality'.

Take a step back from the situation you find yourself in and remember that it will not last forever. Ensure you are keeping a healthy sense of perspective. Try to breathe through it, rather than being consumed by it. You are more than capable of bearing this burden and living to tell the tale. One day, this moment will be nothing but a distant memory. So keep breathing, keep calm, and keep going.

This ordeal will not last forever…you are going to come out the other side soon, I promise! You've got this! Try to live your life with more mindfulness and inner peace. Whatever happens in your life: let it come, let it be, let it go.

72 A JUG FILLS DROP BY DROP

The Buddha once taught that 'a jug fills drop by drop'. This is a wonderful analogy for the importance of having patience! In a society obsessed with 'quick-fixes' and instant gratification, it's so important to remember that genuine and long-lasting transformation takes time. Remember that you don't need to have it all right now! Everything will work out in the end, so take your time and trust in the process!

Instead of hoping for the quick-fix overnight solution, take your time and trust in the process. Try to remember that bigger picture – everything is going to be okay! Remember that the process and the journey are just as important as the final result!

There's absolutely no rush to get to your destination! Take your time and try to enjoy the journey, rather than rushing! You'll get there in the end! It's all going to work out eventually!

So stop rushing and stop believing you need everything in this immediate moment. Trust in the process and take your time! Focus on small steps and marginal gains! Try to enjoy your journey and try to remember that one setback or rejection isn't the end of the world! Believe in the purpose behind your path and take things one step at a time.

Remember: a jug fills drop by drop! So have perseverance and remember the purpose behind what you are doing! There's no need to rush, and there's no need for a 'quick fix' – take your time and enjoy your journey!

73 LIVE YOUR TRUTH

Nothing is more important than living your truth. Nothing matters more than being true to yourself. The 21st century is turning out to be an age of authenticity, individuality, and personal empowerment.

We are living in a world that finally recognises the value and importance of human diversity and personal uniqueness. Our society is finally acknowledging and validating Individual authenticity. People are finally being encouraged to be themselves and flourish as authentic individuals. This is a cause for celebration! And, by living your personal truth, you can contribute to this amazing cause!

Remember this is your one and only lifetime, and so it is essential that you live it to the full. The most effective way of doing this is by aspiring to live your truth. This means being unapologetically authentic and being proud of the unique individual that you are. It means daring to share your story and having the confidence show people your scars, share with them your story, and be open about your authentic journey.

In short, living your truth means courageously creating an authentic, confident, and resilient life. It means stepping outside of your front door with courageousness and vulnerability. And it means wearing what you want, doing what you want, and being whom you want to be as an authentic individual in this world.

Every time you courageously step outside as your most authentic and empowered self, you are inspiring other people to do the same. Just by being authentic, you are becoming an amazing role model and advocate for the next generation. And, just by living as your fearlessly authentic self, you are showing that authenticity is so much more valuable than conformity.

Living your truth requires both confidence and vulnerability. It requires a preparedness to show up, take off the mask you've been hiding behind, and present your most authentic self to the world.

As Brene Brown writes, "Vulnerability sounds like truth and feels like courage. Truth and courage aren't always comfortable, but they're never weakness". Living your truth, whilst undeniably challenging at times, is the most courageous and incredible thing in the world! It is liberating and empowering, both for yourself and also for the people you come into contact with!

So wear your scars with pride and totally own your identity. This is your journey, this is your life, and this is your truth.

Your story is valid. Your truth is powerful. So dare every single day of your life with a real sense of purpose. Be proud of your place in this world. Absolutely own your identity and aspire to inspire the people you meet as you journey through your life on this planet.

Strive to live every single day as your fearlessly authentic self. And proudly live your truth at every possible opportunity. This spirit of authenticity and autonomy is the secret to living your most fulfilling, inspiring and meaningful life imaginable! Dare to be yourself and dare to live your truth!

74 KNOWLEDGE IS POWER

In the words of Francis Bacon, 'knowledge is power'. Therefore, make it your mission to be as informed and educated as you possibly can be! See the world as your classroom and every single day as another opportunity to learn important life lessons!

For thousands of years, philosophers have been warning us to avoid complacency about the extent of our knowledge. As Socrates is quoted as once remarking, 'I know nothing except the fact of my ignorance'. It's clear that what we know in life is a drop, and what we don't know is an ocean.

Education is our most powerful weapon against injustice, discrimination, prejudice and oppression. Through education, we can open minds and enrich lives. Through education, we can liberate the victims of oppression and bring an end to discrimination.

In the words of Kofi Annan: 'Knowledge is power. Information is liberating. Education is the premise of progress, in every society, in every family'. And as the incredibly inspirational Malala Yousafazi says, 'One child, one teacher, one book and one pen can change the world'.

As Toni Payne says, 'knowledge is the new rich…arm yourselves with it'. Nothing is more empowering or enlightening than an education. Nothing is more important for your continued development and wellbeing than reading more, asking more and learning more about the world! Seize every opportunity to broaden your horizons and develop your understanding!

A final word from the Ancient Greek philosopher Socrates, who said this; 'the only good is knowledge, and the only evil is ignorance'. Pursue the goods of knowledge, insight and understanding. Never tire of learning and never tire of expanding your understanding of the universe. Knowledge is power, so arm yourself with wisdom, and you'll be ready to face the world!

75 MAKE FRIENDSHIPS YOUR FOCUS

Strong and loving friendships form the foundations for a fulfilling life. As Aristotle wrote over 2,000 years ago, 'without friends no one would choose to live, though he had all other goods'. Where would we be without our friends? What would we do without our loved ones?

We find purpose in life through our relationships with other people. Our greatest source of happiness is helping, connecting with and caring for other people. Our identity as an individual is grounded in how we interact with people we meet in the world around us. Ultimately, life is all about the people we spend it with. More specifically, life is all about the meaningful connections and loving relationships we form. It's about the support we give, the memories we make, and the moments we share with other people. It's about forging friendships grounded in unconditional love, mutual respect, unwavering trust, and reciprocal altruism.

If you want to live a genuinely happy life, you need to make friendships your focus! You need to make connecting with genuine, kind and honest people your new priority! Every single person you meet in your daily life is a potential friend! One chance encounter at the workplace water cooler could very easily blossom into a lifelong friendship!

Remember, friendships should be based on genuine feelings of connection, closeness and appreciation. Any relationship based on wealth, the position of power, physical attractiveness, or social status is destined for disaster. This kind of superficial and false relationship is deeply toxic for everyone involved! You must be friends with someone because of their heart, values and spirit…not because of their social status! A friendship will only be fulfilling if it is grounded in a genuine appreciation of the other person as an individual.

Your friendship must be anchored by a sense of respect, responsibility, care, and commitment to that person. They can be measured by the amount of unconditional love, and the millions of little gestures, that you both put in. A true friendship will go beyond the superficial and be characterised by a real depth of feeling, care and commitment! Oprah put it perfectly when she said this: "Lots of people want to ride with you in the limo, but what you want is someone who will take the bus with you when the limo breaks down".

Who is there for you when you've taken off your makeup, slipped out of your designer brands and logged out of the social media? Who makes an effort to check in on how you are doing, and who is genuinely happy for you when you succeed? Who is first in the queue to congratulate you for your achievements, and who is first in the queue to wipe away your tears when you're down? Who genuinely cares about you, not what you can offer them? Who would tell you the brutal and honest truth, rather than just saying what they think you want to hear? Who would stand up for you and fight your corner when you were not there, and whose presence genuinely brings joy to your life? Who inspires, empowers, and motivates you to become the very best version of yourself? Whom can you imagine yourself still making memories with in another 10, 20 or even 30 years time?

True and genuine friendship is very hard to find. It is a precious diamond that must be treasured! I won't lie to you: you're going to have to kiss a few frogs on your way to finding this kind of genuine friendship! But, once you've found it, you'll realise that it was worth the wait! Because nothing – and I mean nothing – makes life more fulfilling than genuine friendships! Seek to form these meaningful connections and genuine relationships at every opportunity!

76 COUNT YOUR BLESSINGS

I'm a great believer that gratitude leads to greatness. Indeed, nothing is more enriching or empowering than committing yourself to a life of appreciation and gratitude. When you start approaching life with a spirit of gratitude, your entire life is totally transformed. Your new 'glass-half-full' mentality revolutionises your entire life, leaving you with a real spring in your step every single day of the week!

In a world where everybody always wants more, strive to be somebody who is grateful for every single thing that they have. From the food that you ate for breakfast to the beautiful sunset you witness in the evening, express gratitude for every little thing in your life. Cherish each moment, appreciate life's simple pleasures, and find beauty in the natural world around you. R

alph Waldo Emerson summed up this approach to life like this: "Cultivate the habit of being grateful for every good thing that comes to you and give thanks continuously. And because all things have contributed to your advancement, you should include all things in your gratitude".

At the end of the day, happiness does not come from always wanting more – it is instead the result of appreciating and cherishing everything that you have already got! Instead of always consuming more, why don't we make an effort to consider the value of what we already have? Cherish everything already in your life, from the people you are surrounded by to the simple pleasures that we so easily take for granted. When you start consciously counting your blessings in this way, the quality of your entire life is instantly transformed.

20th-century theologian Dietrich Bonhoeffer put it like this: "In ordinary life, we hardly realise that we receive a great deal more than we give and that it is only with gratitude that life becomes rich".

A 'never enough' mentality is nothing short of soul-destroying. If you cannot be content with what you have now, you will never be content with anything you gain in your entire lifetime. It's not about the material goods; it's about the mindset! Unless you cultivate an internal attitude of appreciation, you will never discover true happiness in your lifetime! Unless you start consciously counting your blessings, you will never feel fulfilled!

As the Ancient Greek philosopher, Epicurus taught over 2,000 years ago: "Do not spoil what you have by desiring what you have not; remember that what you have now was once among the things you only hoped for".

Get serious about counting your blessings! Appreciate every single thing in your life! Start living a life infused with gratitude, and you'll instantly start reaping the rewards! As Charlotte Bronte wrote: "Gratitude is a divine emotion: it fills the heart, but not just to bursting; it warms it, but not to fever".

Don't put off the practice of 'counting your blessings'. Get serious about expressing gratitude for everything you have. Your attitude of gratitude must start right this very second! In the words of James Allen, 'no duty is more important than giving thanks'.

Wherever you go and whatever you do, always count your blessings. Look for reasons to be thankful, and find that the number of things to be thankful for in your life multiplies!

77 TRUST YOUR INTUITION

Never push aside your gut instinct. Never side-line your sixth sense. And never ignore your intuition! I cannot stress how important it is to pay attention to your instincts and intuition! As you make your way through life in this world, always keep 'checking in' on how you feel and always keep paying attention to your 'gut instinct'. If your instincts appear to be telling you something, I'm willing to gamble that they are going to be right!

If you're in a situation and you feel like things don't seem to be adding up, don't side-line that feeling. If you meet someone and something just doesn't seem right about them, don't ignore that gut instinct. #

Your intuition is here to guide, support and assist you as you go about your daily life. Make sure you tune into - and really listen to - your intuition! Don't take it for granted, and don't end up paying the price for ignoring it later down the line!

When your gut tells you something, go with it. When your intuition senses something, listen to it. Become an expert at reading the room, picking up people's vibes, and listening to your intuition. Start going beyond what can be seen with the eye and really listen to what you feel inside. Your gut instinct will rarely be wrong – so give it the attention it deserves.

78 YOU ARE NOT YOUR THOUGHTS

As Aristotle said over 2,000 years ago, 'it is the mark of an educated mind to be able to entertain a thought without accepting it'. One of the most important life skills any of us can ever cultivate is an ability to 'step outside' of our thoughts and consider them as a neutral observer.

Emotional Intelligence is all about becoming aware of our emotions, and I believe that we can extend this practice of conscious awareness to our thoughts and behaviours as well. Living life on 'autopilot' without any awareness of our thoughts and feelings is, to put it frankly, a recipe for disaster.

Without insight into our triggers and fears, we spend our lives repeating the same mistakes, struggling to communicate, and causing both ourselves and loved ones unnecessary amounts of suffering. It is extraordinary to consider how many arguments, outbursts of anger, and acts of self-sabotage could be avoided if only we cultivated intelligent awareness of our own thoughts and feelings.

In order to get better at managing your emotions and making intelligent life decisions, it is essential that you learn to become an observer of your thoughts. It's essential to become aware that not all of your thoughts are necessarily accurate or true.

Many of our fears and worries, for example, have no empirical or justifiable basis whatsoever. Many of our beliefs – about both ourselves and the wider world – are completely irrational and without any logical foundation. It is therefore essential that you don't just accept and believe your thoughts as if they were Biblical truths.

Instead, we must learn to step back and assess them! We must get confident questioning, interrogating and challenging our most deeply held and taken for granted beliefs!

Whenever you find yourself faced with a particularly strong thought, emotion or belief, you've got to ask yourself these key questions: Where is this coming from? Do I have evidence for this? Is this thought, emotion or belief going to help me to live my best life? Is there another perspective or approach that I need to consider? What underlying fears, feelings or insecurities might be influencing my mindset at this moment? Are they helpful, or are they a hindrance to my happiness? What would a neutral observer or therapist have to say about this thought, emotion, or belief?

As you go through life, try to act as your own personal therapist. Never take a single thought, belief or emotion for granted. Instead, interrogate your thoughts and challenge your beliefs.

Take a new perspective on your emotions and see the bigger picture behind your feelings. Remember that you are not your thoughts, emotion, and beliefs – instead, you are an observer and student of them! Learn to observe and – where necessary – challenge your thoughts. See yourself as a scientist who is studying your thoughts in a science lab! Don't be afraid to confront and challenge any irrational beliefs or ideas that you might identify! By taking this intelligent approach to making sense of your thoughts, you can start living your most fulfilling life imaginable!

79 DON'T THINK ABOUT IT, JUST DO IT

Stop putting off that project. Stop delaying your self-improvement. Stop postponing that decision you know needs to be taken and stop stalling on making that major life change. It's very easy to put things off and keep delaying things until tomorrow.

Whilst there may be a good intention behind this, here's the thing you need to know: when you keep delaying everything until tomorrow, tomorrow never comes! And so, it is essential that you stop just dreaming and start actually doing! Instead of just planning and preparing (although these are both very important), make an effort to start actioning and creating!

Why are you delaying until tomorrow something that could have been done today? The longer you delay something, the more doubtful it is you'll ever get it done. The more that you put something off, the more daunting and overwhelming that task appears to look.

Instead of procrastinating and putting something off, roll up your sleeves and dive straight in at the deep end! If you have an idea, then do something about it right now! If you have a dream, then take effective action to turn it into your brand new reality today! If there's something you want or need to do, don't keep delaying it! Bite the bullet, roll up your sleeves, and get down to business!

If something needs starting, then start it right now. Don't delay it for another single second, never mind another day, week or even year! Have a cup of tea, approach the task with confidence, and just go for it! There really is no time like the present! Strike whilst the iron is hot!

80 SELF-DISCIPLINE IS ESSENTIAL FOR SUCCESS

If you want to achieve anything in this world, then you need to get serious about cultivating self-discipline. The more disciplined you get, the easier life gets and the more success you enjoy.

With self-discipline, anything is possible. That's because discipline is the bridge between goals and accomplishments. It allows you to turn your dreams into your reality and, as a result, absolutely transforms your life.

Indeed, your success in life is aligned to your level of discipline and perseverance. The more disciplined you are, the more future success you store up for yourself! The more you practice perseverance right now, the more you will be rewarded greater down the line! Don't just give in to instant gratification – make long-term prosperity your priority!

The 1972 Stanford marshmallow experiment demonstrated the importance of 'delayed gratification' and self-discipline in our lives. The study found that children who were willing to delay gratification (in the study, this meant resisting from eating a marshmallow in order to receive another one later) ended up having higher test scores, lower levels of substance abuse, lower likelihood of obesity, better responses to stress, better social skills, and generally better scores in a range of other life measures.

It is essential that we become capable of sacrificing short-term and instant gratification for the sake of our longer-term success. We need to be strict about our routines and resolve to keep committed to whatever it is we are working on.

Here's what I strongly believe: without self-discipline, you will never get a single thing done in your life…never mind fulfil your potential and become the best version of yourself!

The price of discipline is always less than the pain of regret. Discipline may not always be enjoyable, but it is always profitable. So be strict about sacrificing short-term indulgence for the sake of long-term fulfilment. Stick to your routines and stand firm in your willpower. Be disciplined and be diligent!

Always remember: without short-term sacrifice, there can be no long-term success! If there's one thing that will guarantee you success in life, it's discipline! If you're strict with yourself today, you can guarantee yourself future reward!

Learn to hold your nerve and think long-term. Make an effort to invest in your future success and performance. Instead of wanting it all now, learn to take your time and set yourself up for success later down the line. With no short-term pain, there can be no long-term gain!

81 TRY SOMETHING NEW EVERYDAY

Your comfort zone may be a very comfortable place, but here's the problem: nothing ever grows there! Your comfort zone may feel very safe, but it is not the place where anything magical, extraordinary or amazing happens! And it is therefore not where you belong! As William GT Shedd said, 'A ship is safe in harbour, but that's not what ships are for'.

Dare to step outside of your comfort zone and expand your life! Make it your mission to put yourself out there, do more of the things that scare you, and strive to try something new every single day of your life! See life as an opportunity for learning, progress and self-development.

Stop worrying about what could go wrong and focus your attention on what lessons you'll be able to learn! Keep seizing those opportunities to learn, develop and grow!

Always keep an open mind to trying something new. You never know what doors you might end up opening! Whilst new ways of doing things may seem frightening or unnerving at first, who knows what rewards you might end up reaping?

Dare to leave the safety of your comfort zone behind and get into the life-enhancing habit of trying new things. Get into the habit of thinking outside the box and saying 'yes' to the universe!

Remember that whatever happens, you will be able to handle it. Have the self-confidence to step outside of your familiar territory and dare to try something new!

Remember that, even if it doesn't work out, you will survive! Not only will you survive, but you will grow and learn as an individual thanks to this experience, irrespective of whether the outcomes were good or bad! There is no such thing as failure, only lessons learned!

Make it your mission to try something new every single day. Shake up your routine! Step outside of your comfort zone! Let go of your safety net! Remember that we are only capable of growth, success and flourishing when we are prepared to put ourselves out there and dare to try something different!

Variety, as they say, is the spice of life! Keep trying new things and keep thinking outside the boy! Bring some excitement and self-development into your life! Keep learning and keep enlarging your life as the fearless, resilient and open-minded individual that you were born to be!

82 THE UNIVERSE DOESN'T OWE YOU ANYTHING

It's very easy to go through life with a real chip on your shoulder. Emotions such as envy, anger, frustration and despair are very easy to develop and yet so difficult to shake off. The 'victim mindset' – where you see everything that happens in life as an unfair personal attack on you – is extraordinarily addictive. Once you start blaming the universe for everything that's apparently going wrong in your life, and once you let envy of other people's apparent good fortune become a powerful emotion in your emotional repertoire, it's very hard to get your life back!

Whenever you feel as if the universe is against you or that life just isn't fair, here's what you need to remind yourself: the universe doesn't actually owe you anything. It's a bitter pill to swallow, but it is an essential one all-the-same. The universe does not revolve around you! The world was not created to worship you! Society is not structured so that your every need, wish and desire can be fulfilled! We are all just temporary residents on this planet populated by over 7 billion people.

Whilst our lives have unconditional worth, we don't actually have any right to be here. We need to see life as an incredible gift that we have been extremely fortunate to have received. Every single day that we spend on this planet is a bonus – don't take a single day of your existence for granted! The world was doing perfectly fine before you were born, and the world will keep spinning after you have died. You are, sorry to put it so bluntly, just one tiny drop in the enormous and ever-expanding ocean that is our universe.

We need to remember that the universe does not owe us anything. If things do go well for us in life, then that's truly wonderful! But there is no guarantee or promise that your life is going to be a perfect fairy-tale! Nobody promised you that life was going to be easy! Nobody promised you that your existence was going to be a bed of roses! Remember, the universe does not owe you anything! The universe is not here to fulfil all your wishes and desires!

You have, therefore got to take responsibility for your life by making that commitment to doing the best job that you can with the resources that are available to you.

Don't pray for an easy life; work hard to create a meaningful one! Don't wish that the universe would send you some good fortune…get busy working to guarantee success for yourself! Don't be bitter about the fact that somebody else has had better luck than you. Unfortunately, that's just the way the world works! This is the real world, not some utopian fantasy! Stop complaining and take it on the chin.

Life does not hand us success on a plate. The universe does not owe us an explanation. We are very fortunate to be alive and to exist on this planet – by granting us this existence; the universe has already gone above and beyond for us! So do not take a single thing for granted, and do not complain that your life is not that bed of roses.

You need to radically accept that the universe does not owe you anything. Rather than complaining about the unfairness or injustice of the world, you need to meet the universe where it is now. Work hard to make a success of your life using the resources the world has made available to you.

Remember, nobody promised you that life was going to be easy. Nobody promised you that life was going to be fair. Stop complaining and start taking responsibility for making the best of your circumstances in life! After all, you are the master of your destiny, not the victim of the universe!

83 STAND UP FOR WHAT YOU BELIEVE IN

One of the Buddhist verses of training the mind states this: "as long as space endures, as long as sentient being remain, until then, may I too remain to dispel the miseries of the world". I very strongly believe that we find our purpose in life through the contribution we make to the common good of society. It is when we commit to making a contribution – no matter how big or how small – that we can truly flourish as human beings. That might be caring for your children, donating to a certain charity, pursuing a worthwhile career, or performing random acts of kindness for your neighbours.

One of the most important – and impactful – ways of contributing to the common good of society is standing up for what you believe in. In the democratic world, we are fortunate to have a voice and the right to freedom of speech. In a world where so many people are denied this most basic of human rights, it is essential that we use our voices to speak up and stand up for what we believe in. As the extraordinarily influential Martin Luther King once said, 'Our lives end the day we become silent about things that matter'.

There's an aphorism which says, 'strong people stand up for themselves, stronger people stand up for other people'. See it as your duty and purpose in life to give a voice to the voiceless and to speak out on behalf of those who cannot. Use your platforms – both in-person and online – to stand up for the causes you care about. Give your life a renewed sense of meaning and purpose by speaking out and standing up for what is right.

Christopher Hitchens put it like this: 'Never be a spectator to unfairness or stupidity. The grave will supply plenty of time for silence'. Don't be a sheep whose life is characterised by silence and conformity. If you have the privilege of a voice and a platform, then it is your moral duty to use it on behalf of those who do not. If you want to see a change in society, then you need to dare to become that change. Strive to become the catalyst for progress and transformation. Be selfless and make sacrifices for the greater good of your cause.

Remember that your voice is the most powerful weapon you possess. Make it your mission to use your voice, stand up for what you believe in and make a positive difference. Do what you can to contribute to the common good and leave an inspiring legacy in your wake.

Strive to live a life of integrity and inspiration, not conformity and cowardice. Stand up for what you believe in and speak out on the issues that truly matter. Realise that, in the words of Yasmine Galenorm, 'hate can only exist where people refuse to speak out against it'. As Albert Einstein said, the world will not be destroyed by those who do evil, but by those who watch them without doing anything.

You have a moral duty to stand up for what you believe in. Live with courage, not cowardice. Use your voice and leave a legacy. The final word must go to Martin Luther King Jr, who said this: 'in the end, we will not remember the words of our enemies but the silence of our friends'.

84 TAKE YOUR TIME

The frenetic pace of modern society means so many of us live our lives at 110 miles per hour. In a world of next-day delivery, instant rewards schemes, fast fashion and on-demand movie streaming, everything has to be done with immediacy and urgency. As a result, we run around like headless chickens, exhausting ourselves as we rush from one 'urgent' Everybody is always apparently 'so busy', with 'so much to do and so little time'. It's exhausting just to think about it all!

But really, is there really any need for all of this rushing around? Why does everything have to be so frenetic and fast-paced? Why is there such a need for immediacy and urgency? Does life really have to be lived on this never-ending treadmill of panic, urgency and consumption?

No, of course, it does not! You do not need to have to race through life like some kind of headless chicken! Instead, you can choose to live a much calmer and stable kind of existence. Instead of being so overwhelmed by busyness, you can choose to breathe and take each moment as it comes.

There really is no need to live life at 110 miles per hour. You do not have to spend every single day of your life feeling so stressed, panicked and out of your depth. Instead, you can take your time and take a much more peaceful approach to life! You can choose to do what you can with what you have, rather than spending every day feeling out of your depth and overwhelmed!

Whatever you've got to do, take your time. Stressing about something won't make the outcome anymore successful! If you don't feel calm and at peace in yourself, you cannot reach peak productivity or do your best possible work! Break those overwhelming tasks down and just do what you can. Take it day-by-day and challenge-by-challenge. You have plenty of time to do everything you need and want to do. So don't wish your life away in a blur of stress and despair!

Breathe, take your time, and pace yourself. Do what you can, when you can, with what you have. You are not some kind of superhuman robot! You are not some kind of twenty-four-hour operating machine! Be kind to yourself, remember to breathe, and take your time. You'll get there!

86 GRATITUDE LEADS TO GREATNESS

I'm a great believer that gratitude leads to greatness. Living your life with a spirit of appreciation is guaranteed to boost your mood and raise your vibe! At every opportunity, find something to appreciate! At every moment, look for a reason to be thankful! As Zig Ziglar once said, 'Gratitude is the healthiest of all human emotions. The more you express gratitude for what you have, the more likely you will have even more to express gratitude for!'

Gratitude really is the great multiplier! When you start to appreciate things more, you start attracting more things to be thankful for into your life! In the words of Kristin Armstrong, 'When we focus on our gratitude, the tide of disappointment goes out, and the tide of love rushes in'.

When you go through each day with a grateful heart, you totally transform your existence. Every little thing you once took for granted – such as a cup of tea in the morning – suddenly becomes a moment of luxury in your day. When you start expressing gratitude for all of life's simple pleasures, you start to see that life is so much more enjoyable, fulfilling and fabulous than you ever realised! As Melanie Beattie says, 'Gratitude turns what we have into enough'. An attitude of appreciation will enrich and illuminate your life. It will totally transform the quality of your entire existence!

If you only do one thing today, ensure that it's making a commitment to living with gratitude! Get serious about living with a grateful heart and approaching each day with a spirit of appreciation! Be thankful for everything – both small and big, good and bad – and thank the universe for every opportunity, obstacle, simple pleasure, and life lesson that it sends you!

The last word goes to Rhonda Byrne, who said this: "Gratitude will shift you to a higher frequency, and you will attract much better things". Keep those words in mind as you go through life and appreciate every little thing!

87 STAND UP FOR YOURSELF

Always stand up for yourself. Don't let anybody walk all over you! If somebody is intentionally trying to put you down, don't you dare put up with it!

I am a strong believer that, in life, you only get what you put up with. And that means you do not have to tolerate anybody intentionally being rude, malicious or hateful towards you! It is, of course, just a fact of life that there are people in this world who wouldn't think twice before walking all over you or throwing you under a bus. These people, who are typically lacking in empathy and emotional intelligence, lack the capacity to consider how their actions might impact you.

These self-obsessed people are so caught up in their own selfish needs and desires that they are unable to consider – or care about - how you might be hurt or upset by the way they are treating you. Sometimes, they are so unhappy in themselves that they actually think they'll feel better about themselves if they cause somebody else harm. As they pursue their selfish personal desires, believe in their own delusions of grandeur and try to escape their state of deep self-hatred, they will try to walk all over you or use you as a means for fulfilling their personal needs.

I use the word 'try' very intentionally, because nobody can ever put you down without your permission to do so. As Eleanor Roosevelt is believed to have once said, 'No one can make you feel inferior without your consent'. Let me be very clear: if somebody is intentionally putting you down or causing you harm, you do not have to put up with it!

Nobody can ever take away your intrinsic worth and value as a human being. Someone might take away your physical possessions or treat you in an appalling manner, but they can never take away that intrinsic value.

Michael J Fox puts it like this: 'One's dignity may be assaulted, vandalised and cruelly mocked, but it can never be taken away unless it is surrendered'. And you should not – under any circumstances – ever surrender that dignity. Your worth is unconditional, and your dignity is unquestionable. So do not let anybody make you feel worthless or inferior! Every single human being on this planet is equal and deserves to be treated with nothing less than absolute respect. No matter what they do or say, nobody can ever take your intrinsic worth and value away.

Here's what I want to ask: do you deserve to be put down, mistreated or used as a means to an end? Of course, you don't! And guess what? You don't have to be! Whilst you cannot force people to respect you, you can refuse to be disrespected.

Do not be afraid to stand up for yourself and speak up for what is right. If somebody is intentionally putting you down, don't you dare put up with it! They can take away your possessions and maybe even your freedoms, but they can never take away your dignity and value as a human being. Never forget your unconditional worth and never be afraid to stand up for yourself. At all times, know your worth!

88 LIVE WITH A TOUGH MIND AND A TENDER HEART

Live your life with a tough mind and a tender heart. As Martin Luther King Jr once famously said, 'We must combine the toughness of the serpent and the softness of the dove, a tough mind and a tender heart'. King was taking inspiration from Jesus Christ, who had taught his disciples to be as 'wise as serpents and as harmless as doves'.

Jesus, observed King, recognised the need for blending opposites. Jesus did not like with his head in the clouds; he knew that his disciples would face a difficult and hostile world, and he knew that they would encounter cold and arrogant men. In order to spread their message of love, forgiveness and justice, they needed to live with a tough mind and a tender heart. They needed the mental strength to stand up for what was right and , but they needed the tenderness of heart in order to remain kind and compassionate no matter what the world threw at them!

In our lives, we need to strike this balance of a tough mind and a tender heart. We need to have the courage and conviction to stand up for what is right, but we must also never become hardened by the setbacks and struggles that come from living in an often selfish and unfair world. Our minds must be tough and yet our hearts must remain tender! It's a very tricky balancing act, but it's one that we are all capable of pulling off!

89 BE THE CHANGE

It was Gandhi who once famously said: "be the change you wish to see in the world". Do you ever find yourself despairing at the circumstances you encounter in the world? Do you ever wish that things could be different in our society? Well, what is actually stopping you from actively bringing about that change you wish to see in the world?

Whenever you encounter any type of injustice or whenever you realise that there is an absence of something in society, you shouldn't just complain about it. Instead, you should actively aspire to do something about it! You should, in other words, resolve to *be the change you wish to see in the world!*

We find meaning in our lives by making a difference in the world and contributing to the common good of society. Strive to create a genuinely meaningful life by becoming an architect of change in this world. Take responsibility for making a real difference on the issues that matter to you, and dedicate your life to making this world a better place.

Remember: never just complain about something or wish that things could be different – actively become the change and take responsibility for making that transformation happen! Make your mark, leave your legacy, and make a positive contribution to the common good. This, after all, is what life is all about!

90 DON'T PUT ALL YOUR EGGS IN ONE BASKET

Have you ever heard that old saying, 'don't put all of your eggs in one basket'? I don't think there's ever been a truer word spoken! Whilst it's important to put your heart and soul into everything that you do, and whilst it is essential that you pursue your passions with every ounce of enthusiasm in your body, you must make sure your life is never consumed with one single thing.

It's a very risky business to invest all of your time and energy into one single thing or one area of your life. Imagine, for example; you spend your entire life obsessing about dating and relationships. If you spend all of your time talking about dating – to the extent that it becomes the predominant topic of all your conversations - then what on earth will you talk about when you are finally in a relationship? And if your entire life is spent glued to the side of your partner, what would be left in your life if you ever broke up with them?

Or perhaps it's your job that has become the be-all and end-all of your existence ... how will you cope if the company goes bust or you're suddenly made redundant? It is essential that we do not over-invest in one single area of life but that we instead create a balanced and diverse existence! in other words, it is essential that we become people of substance with a wide variety of interests passions and pastimes.

Imagine your life like an equally balanced pie-chart, made up of lots of different slices! Don't let one interest or topic totally consume your entire existence! Instead, maintain a healthy balance of several! This means that we will not become dependent on one single thing or one single person for all of our validation and success. Instead, our existence will become enriched by an eclectic pallet of different pursuits. And so, even if one thing is suddenly lacking in our lives, we will have a healthy variety of other passions remaining. In other words, life will go on!

The same applies to how we spend our time. Try not to let one task totally consume you! Make sure you make time for plenty of different tasks and activities every single day! Schedule in time for focused work as well as relaxation! Try to maintain a manageable routine, enabling you to live your life as the best version of yourself without burning out!

Always remember that balance is everything! Strive to create a life that resembles something like a well-structured pie chart, with a fulfilling and enriching variety of people, interests, and pursuits! Instead of putting all your eggs in one basket, enrich your life by ditching the dependency and cultivating greater diversity!

91 SAY YES TO THE UNIVERSE!

Stop holding yourself back. Stop worrying about what could go wrong. Stop worrying about what other people might think. Remember, whatever happens in life, you can handle it! And remember, what other people think of you is none of your business! The only thing you should be concerned with is self-growth and personal development!

With that in mind, I want you to make saying yes your new priority. Open yourself up to experiencing success and enlarging your life! Allow the universe to bring new opportunities and experiences into your world! The next time someone asks you out, or you are given the opportunity to do something, I want you to just say yes. Don't worry about what could go wrong, don't let your insecurities tell you that you're going to end up making a fool of yourself! Instead of listening to those self-limiting beliefs, dare to say yes and give it a go!

Just ask yourself this: what's actually the worst thing that can happen? Remember, even if everything goes wrong, you'll have learned a great life lesson! As the old saying goes, we only ever regret the chances we didn't take! So forget your faith, move beyond yourself doubt, and just say yes! Don't think about it; just put yourself out there and give it a go! Every single time we say yes - especially to something that feels outside of our comfort zone - we instantly enrich and expand our lives. by saying yes, we can learn, grow, and thrive like never before! You never know what opportunities your next 'yes' might lead to. You never know what doors might be opened simply because you dared to say 'yes' to something!

So stop depriving yourself of personal growth and opportunities for success! Replace your fear of what could go wrong with a confident conviction that whatever ever happens, you will be able to handle it! The next time someone asks you out or gives you an opportunity, don't think about it…just say yes! Allow the universe to enlarge your life! Take risks, open doors, and guarantee yourself that personal growth! You are much stronger than you realise! So give it a go, put yourself out there, and dare to enlarge your life! Who knows what might happen and what doors might be opened…

92 KILL THEM WITH KINDNESS

Kindness is the most powerful weapon in the world. At all times, love and compassion reign supreme. No matter what you are up against in life, always know that your most powerful ally is the power of kindness. As Immanuel Kant once said 'goodness shines forth like a precious jewel'. Kindness is the supreme human virtue, guaranteed to illuminate your life and overcome absolutely any hostility or adversity that you may be confronted with.

Whilst people may gain temporary power through unsavoury actions or outbursts, the only eternally enduring force is goodness. And goodness is best demonstrated through the three supreme virtues of love, kindness, and compassion. If you are ever confronted with hostility or adversity, please be assured that the most powerful weapon in your repertoire is your kindness. With love, kindness and compassion, you are an unstoppable force for good.

As the eternally inspiring St Paul writes, 'Love does not delight in evil but rejoices with the truth. It always protects, always trusts, always hopes, always perseveres'. Love, kindness, and compassion are the three most powerful and enduring forces in the world. Never underestimate their power; they will always prevail and come out on top, no matter what evil forces they may be up against.

Whatever happens, keep believing in the power and importance of kindness. Realise that love, kindness and compassion will never let you down.

If you want to be a winner in life, you need to get serious about the importance of kindness. No matter what anybody says or does, always respond to them with kindness and love.

Kindness is the most powerful and enduring force known to mankind. It overcomes all obstacles and undermines anyone who may wish to cause you harm. As Abraham Lincoln once said, 'I destroy my enemies when i make them my friends'. And in the words of St Paul: 'Do not be overcome by evil, overcome evil with good'. Whatever happens, goodness will always reign supreme. So believe in the supreme power of kindness, and kill your enemies with a smile.

93 USE SOCIAL MEDIA RESPONSIBLY

Social media has completely revolutionised the way we live our lives. Millions of us now spend countless hours a day scrolling through social media apps, engaging with an endless stream of content and communicating with people all over the world.

Whilst social media has undoubtedly benefited our lives and enriched our society, it is not without its risks and problems. If we do not use social media in an intelligent and responsible way, there is a risk that online platforms could end up causing us more harm than good.

In an online world of fake news, fake followers and artificially enhanced appearances, we need to be strict about how we use social media. Primarily, we need to ensure that social media is serving us in a positive way, rather than letting ourselves become slaves to the social media. Realise that social media companies are multi-billion dollar businesses – all that they are doing is trying to make money and sell you a product!

Only keep using social media products as long as they are enhancing your experience of the real world! For example: does social media help you to communicate with your loved ones? Does social media help you to market your business? Does social media provide you with inspiration, motivation, and empowerment? Only keep logging into your social media apps if they are enhancing and improving the quality of your life! Don't let social media become your entire life!

 And don't mistake the online world of We need to be very clear about the fact that social media is not the real world, but merely one of many different tools we can use in order to communicate, share content, and connect with other human beings.

Whenever you engage with a social media platform, you need to see it for what it is. You need to be very clear with yourself that most of what you see is not an accurate reflection of life in the real world. Images and information found online are not necessarily accurate. Social media 'followers' can never compensate to real life relationships or connections. The way in which someone appears online is not necessarily the way they appear in the real world.

You cannot live your life on social media. What you see and engage with online does not necessary reflect real life! You need to escape the toxic trap of social media addiction and be very clear about your intentions for going online! Have boundaries, be real with yourself, and only use social media if it benefits you. Do not become a slave to social media companies, who are nothing more than businesses trying to make themselves lots of money!

The CEOs of the world's top social media companies all limit the amount of screen-time their own children have. They're all too aware that social media carries many risks if it is not used in an intelligent way! Social media should be a tool to help you live, not the reason you live!

Do not live your life through social media, and do not think that what you see on social media is real life! Most people's Instagram feeds are no more realistic than a Disney movie! Social media only ever shows you the very tip of the iceberg! As long as you're aware of this, you're absolutely fine to use social media to your heart's content. As long as you use it intelligently, there's no need to worry about your use of social media.

Don't fall into the trap of overinvesting in your social media. See social media for what it is (a tool that can serve us) rather than letting it become an all-consuming presence in your life. Be strict about your screen time and be clear about the boundaries between social media and real life.

At all times, remember this: the virtual world is not the real world. Only use social media if it helps you to live a better life in the real world. It should serve you a positive purpose, rather than becoming the entire purpose of your whole existence. Social media is a 'means to an end', not the end in itself.

For the sake of your mental health and wellbeing, make a commitment to using social media responsibly. For the sake of your real-world success, make sure you set boundaries for your use of social media! Only keep scrolling as long as it serves you a positive purpose! Only engage with content that inspires, empowers, and improves you as a human being!

Don't take your social media too seriously! Instead, use your social media in an intelligent, responsible and life-enhancing way. This means seeing it for what it is, rather than letting it ruin your life!

94 BE A GOOD LISTENER

You have two ears and one mouth…learn to use them in that proportion! In a world where everybody has so much to say, it takes a very wise individual to realise that you learn and gain so much more by listening!

Listening – an artform which is a lot harder than it looks – is life-changing. Just by listening to someone, you can support them in ways that no amount of money or material assistance could. When we listen to someone – without judgement and without imposition – we bring them an immeasurable amount of happiness and healing. Just by giving someone our full attention and taking in what they have to say, we can soothe their soul and release them from the burdens of whatever they're battling with in their life. Listening is the most amazing and transformative practice in the world, benefitting both you and the person you are actively listening to!

At the heart of being a good listener lies the fundamental value of empathy. Empathy, defined by the Oxford dictionary as 'the ability to understand and share in the feelings of another', is all about placing yourself in someone else's shoes. Empathy is about understanding what someone is going through or experiencing from within their frame of reference, allowing you to develop understanding and compassion for that person.

Empathy goes to the core of what it means to be a human being. It enriches our lives by opening our hearts and enriching our lives. And the best way to cultivate this all-important empathy is by becoming a good listener. Take time to hear people's stories and give your full attention to whatever they have to say. When someone speaks, shares their story or shares their problems with you, make sure you give them your full attention. Try to fully engage with what they are saying, giving them the time and attention to really open up and express themselves.

As I say, in a world where everyone has so much to say, finding a good listener is like finding a needle in the haystack! There are lots of books on social skills and social confidence. They teach us how to be interesting or how to engage someone. I think the most important lesson in social skills is this: in life, you should strive to be interested, rather than interesting.

By which I mean, strive to take a genuine interest in every single person that you meet. Instead of worrying about what they might think of you, take a sincere and genuine interest in their life. Ask them questions, and then really listen to their answers. Give them your attention and let them share their story.

Get into the habit of asking genuine questions, and then really listening to the answers people give you! Give people your full attention, ask to follow up questions where relevant, and remember key details people choose to share with you! When you listen to someone - without trying to make the conversation all about you - you make someone feel like they're worth a million dollars! And people will never forget how you have made them feel! Just by taking an active interest in someone's life - and really listening to what they say - you can make someone's day!

Seize every opportunity to learn more about the world by hearing about people's stories, opinions, perspectives, and experiences! Not only will it make them feel amazing, but it will enrich your life as well! Listening to someone doesn't take anything away from your life...it just improves and enhances it!

In a world where people think shouting loudest is the only way to stand out, the person who can nonjudgmentally listen to others is a very valuable person indeed! And not only that, but they will become a very wise, intelligent and desirable person as well!

Strive to make someone's day, every day...just by listening to what they've got to say! Just by simply asking questions, and really listening to the answers, we can change people's lives...and our own as well! Every single person we meet has something interesting to teach us. Every single human being has a unique story to share. Listening to people will not only boost *their* wellbeing, but it will also teach you so much as well.

Just by listening to someone, you can genuinely make their day...and may even change their life! Just by listening to someone, you can bring them hope, healing and genuine happiness. Just by listening to someone's story or giving them space to talk through what they're going through, you can make the most positive difference in their life. Never underestimate the power and importance of being a good listener!

95 PRIORITISE INTEGRITY OVER POPULARITY

"It's nice to be liked, but it's better to be respected". Integrity, I have to tell you, is so in this season. Integrity is so in every season! Whilst popularity and attention will come and go in waves; integrity is an essential constant in your life. Popularity ends on yearbook day, whereas respect will last forever.

In a society obsessed with influencers, trends and viral videos, we can often forget about the importance of integrity. As we chase after the next trend or seize the next opportunity to become popular, it can become all too easy to forget about our integrity as individuals. Neglecting your integrity is a major mistake. Because whilst popularity may bring you a short-term hit of pleasure, only integrity can bring you long-term fulfilment and success in this world.

Unlike popularity or 'being on-trend', which come in very short term and unreliable waves, integrity has endurance and can be sustained through life's many storms. It will anchor and sustain you no matter what is happening in the world around you, providing you with a secure identity and lifelong social success.

Integrity does not depend on how popular you are in a certain social setting or on many 'likes' you might get on a social media platform. Just because something is popular that doesn't mean it is morally right. Just because someone has popularity – or, as is often the case, notoriety – that doesn't mean they have happiness or fulfilment in life. Indeed, a lifetime spent chasing popularity and social approval lead to a very insecure and unfulfilling existence.

Think about it: Do you really want to spend your life chasing short-term moments of popularity? Is this life of desperation, insecurity and uncertainty really what you want? Or would you prefer long-term fulfilment and flourishing as a stable, secure, and respected individual?

Julius Erving put it like this: 'I firmly believe that respect is a lot more important, and a lot greater than, popularity'. And Eric Harvey said this: 'Courage is following your conscience instead of following the crowd'.

Margaret Chase Smith said, 'Standing for right when it is unpopular is a true test of moral character'. This is especially relevant in a populist and social media dominated society. It's easy to stand with the crowd, but living a life ruled by conformity will do nothing but destroy your soul. If you want true success and flourishing in this lifetime, make living with integrity your brand new priority.

Integrity is all about rising above popular opinion and living an autonomous life. It means standing up for what is right, even if that doesn't make you popular right now. It means being true to yourself and living in accordance with your core values, rather than compromising on your principles for the sake of gaining short-term popularity. Integrity means being prepared to sacrifice short-term attention or popularity for the greater good of both your soul and the common good of society.

At all times, conduct yourself with integrity. Don't sell your soul for the sake of some short-term attention! Stay true to your core values and command the respect that you deserve! Laurence Sterne believed this: 'Respect for ourselves guides our morals; respect for others guides our manners'. Make integrity your priority and make respect your key currency!

Remember that integrity is fashionable 365 days a year. Whilst trends and popularity will come and go; respect will last a lifetime.

96 SPEAK TO PEOPLE IN A LANGUAGE THEY UNDERSTAND

Effective communication is the key to successful relationships in every area of our lives. And the secret to effective communication is speaking to people in a language that they understand. This means learning to adapt and tailor our ways of communicating and talking to our audience, conveying our message in a way that the people we are speaking to will understand.

Nelson Mandela once famously said this: 'If you talk to a man in a language that he understands, that goes to his head. If you talk to him in his language, that goes to his heart'. If we want to form meaningful connections, we need to learn how to communicate more intelligently. There is no 'one size fits all' when it comes to conveying a message - we need to understand that different people communicate in different ways. If we want to enjoy fruitful and successful interpersonal relationships, we need to learn how to 'read the room' and adapt our communication style to the needs of our audience.

As the 20th-century philosopher, Ludwig Wittgenstein said, 'the limits of my language are the limits of my world'. People 'only know what they have words for'. In order to excel in the different social contexts we find ourselves in as human beings, we need to get confident at 'code-switching', which means learning to adapt to those different social contexts we find ourselves in.

Each of us is constantly participating in different 'language games', within which the language we use shapes our world view. Whenever you arrive into a new social context or new interpersonal relationship – and so a new language game – you must play by the rules and norms of that particular game. In other words, you must speak to people in a language that they understand!

We need to study communication at both an individual and a social level. Every single person has a unique style of communication and self-expression. If we want to connect with someone, we need to make an effort to understand their unique communication style.

In his revolutionary book 'The Five Love Languages: How to Express Heartfelt Commitment', Gary Chapman outlines five different ways that romantic partners express and experience love. These are - acts of service, gift-giving, physical touch, quality time, and words of affirmation. In his book, Chapman writes about the importance of discovering people's 'love languages' through observing the ways that they express love, analysing what they complain about most often, and reflecting on what they seem to be wanting/requesting from their romantic partners.

Chapman hypothesised that each person has one 'primary' love language as well as one 'secondary' love language. And so, by understanding our own – and our partners – love languages, we can become better communicators and so, as a result, enjoy better relationships!

Different people express themselves and communicate their feelings in very different ways. We need to get intelligent about understanding different people's methods of communication. We need to cultivate empathy for the different methods of self-expression and communication that people use. When someone expresses themselves in a way that we are not familiar with, it can be easy to take the signals or messages they are sending in the wrong way.

That's why we need to learn how to read other people's communication styles, as well as gain some insight into our own! We need to learn how to stop signalling our feelings and hoping people will pick up on them and learn how to explicitly express them much more clearly instead (e.g. through explicitly telling someone how we are feeling).

Whenever you find yourself forming a new connection or in a new social context, make it your mission to become a student of other people's communications. Work out what language they speak and identify the ways in which they signal their emotions, feelings, and needs. Do they say how they are feeling or communicate their emotions through more subtle signals? What does their body language reveal about their emotions at this moment? How might their emotions, insecurities, fears and desires be driving the things that they do and say?

Strive to become an expert communicator! Learn how to 'read the room' and tailor your message to your audience. Study your own 'love languages' and become a student of other people's as well! Learn how to effectively get your message across to different types of communicators and learn how to pick up on the subtle signals and subconscious messages people send out as they interact in the world!

96 BEAUTY COMES FROM WITHIN

The contents of your heart matters so much more than your appearance in the mirror. Whilst physical attractiveness is very superficial and skin-deep, true beauty comes from within.

A beautiful heart creates a beautiful person. Your physical appearance does not determine your true beauty as a human being. Of course, it might make you physically appealing or sexual desirable. And, you know what they say, if you've got it...flaunt it! But physical attractiveness is nowhere near equivalent to the true beauty that comes from within. True beauty is all about the contents of your head and the spark within your soul. It is not measured by your facial features, height, or waistline. Instead, it is measured by your kindness, compassion and human spirit. Beauty isn't about having a pretty face or Instagram-perfect appearance. Instead, beauty is about having a pretty mind, a pretty soul, and a pretty heart.

Elisabeth Kubler Ross puts it beautifully: 'People are like stained glass windows. They sparkle and shine when the sun is out, but when the darkness sets in, their true beauty is revealed only if there is a light from within'. Whilst the makeup, six pack and beach body are fabulous, what is left when you look beyond these physical features? You can only be said to have true beauty if you have a beautiful heart and a beautiful soul deep within you.

Remember, true beauty always comes from within! It's about that gorgeous heart and loving soul within you! In the words of one of my favourite philosophers Immanuel Kant, 'good shines forth like a precious jewel'. So let your goodness sparkle bright!

Beauty is all about having a beautiful heart and a beautiful soul. Beauty comes from being somebody who makes everybody feel like a somebody. It comes from living an unashamedly authentic, kind, and loving life. Beauty is a heart of gold paired with a stardust soul. Dare to look beyond the superficial, and realise that beauty is all about shining from within.

97 DON'T TAKE YOURSELF TOO SERIOUSLY

Too many of us take ourselves far too seriously. We approach trivial issues like they are matters of life and death and endlessly worry about things that, in reality, do not matter. We are so anxious about how we look to other people that we are terrified of letting our hair down, kicking off our shoes, and having a fair bit of fun! I believe that to live your best life, a good sense of humour is essential! A good sense of humour not only makes you more likeable to other people, but it also means that you will like YOURSELF more!

When you have a good sense of humour, you are no longer anxious about being laughed at or worried about making a fool of yourself. When you start living a life filled with laughter, your paralysing fear of being embarrassed or making mistakes is extinguished overnight. I strongly believe that life presents us with two obvious choices. We can choose either to take everything seriously and walk around on eggshells, or we can decide to live with a sense of humour and laugh our way through every day!

Here's the thing - As long as you are alive, you have no excuse not to be laughing your way through every little 'setback' and 'blooper' that you face! People love someone who can entertain them, and the most entertaining people are those who can make a joke - and take a joke - at their own expense.

You should therefore strive to become secure enough in your skin that you can make a joke about your misfortunes and crack a joke about the flaws in your personality. Don't be so sensitive and serious about everything – have a laugh and share a smile! Nothing is that deep. Whatever has gone wrong today will almost certainly be forgotten about by tomorrow. So lighten up and lighten your load! Have a laugh at your own expense and start enjoying life so much more!

98 ALWAYS LOOK ON THE BRIGHT SIDE OF LIFE

Always look on the bright side of life! Always see the funny side of every situation, no matter how serious it may seem! At the end of the day, nothing is really that deep. Do you really need to lose sleep over that petty argument or trivial situation? Do you really need to take that incident as if it was a matter of life or death? As long as you are still alive, you are still capable of laughing and seeing the funny side of the situation. And, for the sake of your happiness and sanity, it is essential that you do just that!

Yes, life is unfair. Yes, people let us down. Yes, the world can seem very cruel and heartless. We know that life is tough, and we know that you didn't deserve half of the things that happened to you. But here's the thing: does constantly complaining and feeling like a victim of life actually help you in any way, shape or form?

No matter what has happened in life, we always have the power to choose our mindset and outlook. As the inspirational Holocaust survivor Viktor Frankl once famously wrote, 'Everything can be taken away from a man but one thing: the last of the human freedoms – to choose one's attitude in any given circumstances, to choose one's own way'. That's right: you retain, at all times, complete autonomy over your mindset and mental disposition.

I, therefore, encourage you to approach life with a glass-half-full mentality. For every complaint we have about our lives, there is always something we can appreciate. Just the fact that you are alive and can breathe fresh air is amazing! Try to see every challenge as a chance for some self-growth and personal development. Try to see every obstacle as an opportunity to become a more empathetic and resilient individual. Even if you have lost absolutely every single possession you own, just be thankful that you have still got your life.

When it rains, look for rainbows. When it's dark, look for stars. Strive to appreciate every single thing in your life. Nothing is so small that it doesn't deserve our gratitude or appreciation. Seth Godin puts it like this: 'Optimism is the most important human trait because it allows us to evolve our ideas, to improve our situation, and to hope for a better tomorrow'.

As long as you are alive, you have complete autonomy over your mentality! And so, you are capable of choosing to be optimistic. As long as you are breathing, you are capable of appreciating every single breath you take. Try to approach even the most challenging situations with a spirit of self-depreciation and a good sense of humour.

Keep things in perspective, and don't lose sight of what's really important in life. Remain hopeful, be optimistic, and laugh your way through each day. A good sense of humour really is the best medicine, so always try to look on the bright side of life!

99 SMILE AND THE WORLD WILL SMILE BACK

Never underestimate the power and importance of a smile. It is the most simple – and yet most powerful – of human gestures! There is not a single social situation that cannot be instantly improved by a smile. With just one smile, you can light up a room, bring warmth to any social situation, and transform someone's day!

Smiling is a universally recognisable signal of human warmth and goodwill. It transcends all cultural barriers and personal differences. With just one smile, you can make somebody's day. With just one smile, you can even change the world. As Steve Maraboli says, 'smile at strangers, and you might change a life'. Who would have thought that such a simple facial movement could have such a transformative impact?

Smiling changes both your outlook on life, as well as other people's outlook on you. With a smile on your face, you exude nothing but friendliness, confidence, and goodwill. With a smile on your face, every life you touch turns to gold! Use your smile to change the world; don't let the world change your smile. Everywhere you go, make it your mission to smile at as many people as you can. Remember that with just one smile, you can light up a room, make someone's day, and illuminate the world. Smiling will not only change the lives of the people you see and interact with, but it will also change your own life as well. I really do believe that you can smile your worries, anxieties and fears away!

Smiling is so simple and yet so effective. Never tire of giving each person you meet – whether they are a stranger or your soulmate – your brightest and most beautiful smile. And that starts with yourself! When you look in the mirror each morning, make sure you give yourself your biggest and brightest smile! And then, go out into the world with that beaming smile glowing on your face, and shine!

100 A LITTLE BIT OF WHAT YOU FANCY DOES YOU GOOD!

An essential part of living a balanced life is remembering that a little bit of what you fancy does you good! If we don't get a balance of work, rest and play, we cannot flourish or fulfil our potential as human beings!

If we just work, we will burn out and find that life becomes a chore. And if we just play, we will soon find our lives to be very unstimulating and unfulfilling. That's why balance is key! And that's why it's so important to regularly treat yourself and make time for the things that you enjoy!

In order to enjoy success in life, learning how to switch off is absolutely essential! In the same way that you schedule in time for work, you need to schedule in time for relaxation and release! That means pencilling in time for watching your favourite TV shows, reading good books, going out for drinks, and doing all of the things that you enjoy…without feeling in the slightest bit guilty!

Whilst hard work is important, so is getting plenty of rest and recreation. You need time to recharge and let off some steam! You need time to just enjoy yourself, without worrying about what you've got to do or what responsibilities you might have. Never feel guilty about taking some 'me time', and remember that treating yourself to a little bit of what you fancy does you good!

So stop depriving yourself, punishing yourself and pushing yourself twenty-four hours of the day! Make time for doing nothing, winding down, and indulging! Enjoy those simple pleasures and savour those little luxuries in your day.

101 KEEP YOUR FACE TOWARDS THE SUNSHINE

Yes, I know life can be tough. Yes, I know that times can be hard. However, I also know that, even in the darkest times, hope and goodness can be found... If only we are prepared to look for it! Even in the bleakest of moments, there are still things we can be thankful for. For example, the fact that we are alive a something we should never take for granted! and so, even in those darkest of moments, we can still appreciate the gift that is our existence.

In those toughest of times, try to keep your eyes and attention fixed on the light that is ahead of you. Remember, there is always light at the end of the tunnel. Remember, there is always hope on the horizon. As Desmond Tutu says, 'hope is being able to see that there is light, despite all of the darkness'.

Never lose hope and never lose sight of the sunshine. Be grounded in gratitude for the gift of your life, and be inspired by the promise of brighter times ahead. Those clouds will clear, and sunshine will illuminate your life once more. Try to keep focused on the good and try to keep going! Keep moving forwards and never lose hope. Tomorrow will be a brighter day! Goodness will always prevail! Whatever you are going through right now, always have hope for tomorrow!

Keep your face towards the sunshine and put your faith in the power of love, goodness, light and hope. Whatever happens today, always have hope for tomorrow. Be optimistic and look towards the light! No matter what you're going through, always endeavour to keep going, keep growing and keep working to become the best version of yourself! Life may be tough, my dear friend, but you are tougher!

Whatever you're going through right now, keep going. Keep daring to dream big, spread love, and inspire the people around you! Keep your face towards the sunshine, and dare to live your most fearlessly authentic, confident, and resilient life!

AFTERWORD

Thank you so much for taking the time to read this little collection of mantras – I hope you might take away one or two pieces of wisdom and motivation for your everyday life!

It would be wonderful to hear from you on social media – please get in touch on Instagram, TikTok or send me an email to benwardlebooks@gmail.com!

May I just take this opportunity to wish you every success in your year ahead. May you dare to live your most authentic, confident, and resilient life! May you dare to turn obstacles into opportunities and may you dare to 'feel the fear...and do it anyway'!

At all times, remember that you are loved and have unconditional worth. Remember that it's okay not to be okay, and know that whatever happens in your life...you can handle it! So dare to live your best life, and endeavour to enjoy every step of the journey!

Wherever you go and whatever you do, remember that authenticity is the most attractive thing you can wear. Whatever happens, remember that you can handle it. Be kind to yourself and be kind to every single person that you meet. You've got this!

Until next time, may God bless you and your loved ones. Keep shining, keep growing and keep glowing!

With all my love,

Ben

December 2020 | benwardle.org

GET IN TOUCH

I would absolutely love to hear from you!

Instagram: @benwardle_ / @benwardlebooks

Twitter: @benwardle_

Email: benwardlebooks@gmail.com

Join my mailing list at www.benwardle.org

---

101 Mantras for Life is written and published by BEN WARDLE

BENWARDLE.ORG

Printed in Great Britain
by Amazon

55303949R00102